A
Brother
Like Me

About the Author

HARRY B. DUNBAR, a native of Mineola, New York, grew up in and attended public schools in communities on New York's Long Island and in its Hudson Valley. He holds B.S., M.A., and Ph.D. degrees, all from New York University, with concentrations in French Language and Literature. He is Professor Emeritus of Humanities of New York City Technical College of the City University of New York and was Dean of Faculty at Bergen Community College in Paramus, New Jersey. He is a Life Member of Alpha Phi Alpha Fraternity, Inc., and a Life Member of the NAACP.

Harry B. Dunbar

A Brother Like Me

A Memoir

Queenhyte
WILMINGTON

THIS IS A QUEENHYTE BOOK

Copyright © 1995 by Harry B. Dunbar. All rights reserved under International and Pan-American Copyright Conventions. Published in the United States by Queenhyte Publishers, Wilmington, Delaware. Distributed by North Coast Associates, 119 Rockland Center, Suite 320, Nanuet, NY 10954.

Design & composition by C+S GOTTFRIED.
Printing and binding by BookCrafters.

ISBN 0-9643654-0-5

Library of Congress Cataloging-in-Publication Data

Dunbar, Harry B. A Brother Like Me: A Memoir / by Harry B. Dunbar - 1st ed.
p. ; cm.
Includes index.
ISBN 0-9643654-0-5
1. Dunbar, Harry B. - Childhood and Youth. 2. Service in the US Army in World War II. 3. College Years. 4. College Teacher in Mississippi and Arkansas. 5. Graduate School Years and Teacher in New York Public Schools. 6. Fellowship Year in Paris. 7. Teacher in NYC Suburbs and Engagement in the Civil Rights Movement. 8. Professor and Dean at New York City Community College. 9. Dean at Bergen Community College in New Jersey.

CIP # 94-61310

Manufactured in the United States of America

First Edition

Contents

Foreword	*ix*
Acknowledgments	*xiii*
1. By Their Fruit You Shall Know Them	1
2. Under the Colors	25
3. Apprenticeship to the Life of the Mind	45
4. Sojourn in the Confederacy, 1949–1954	55
5. Full Man, Ready Man, Exact Man	69
6. Sojourn in the Fifth Republic	81
7. Engagement to the Cause	89
8. Alpha Comes to Rockland County	109
9. An Examined Life	127
10. Introspection	149
11. Preparing for Retirement	165
12. Detour to Bergen Community College	175
13. Rewriting History	193
Epilogue	199
Notes	201
Bibliography	223
Index	230

This book is dedicated to the memories of my father, Shafter Nathan Dunbar, and my mother, Elma Alexandria Russell-Brown Dunbar, who together charted the course, navigated the ship and piloted it through the dangerous straits of Scylla and Charybdis.

Foreword

This memoir was written twenty-five years after a group of students set me to thinking about how my views squared or did not square with theirs on matters relating to blacks. I conceived it to establish a written record of my beliefs, positions and recollections regarding the issues and events that I confronted or witnessed during my life and career. In it I recognize, underline and emphasize the importance of the contributions of my parents and my siblings to my development into whatever it is that I have become. The meandering, Proustian and Tocquevillean nature of the writing is inevitable; it attempts to be chronological and is as accurate as is possible when many events are recalled through the prism of the passage of as many as sixty years.

This memoir was not written in the same way that my doctoral dissertation was written, that is, by developing and testing a hypothesis. Rather, I took as a starting point the serious wonderment of a group of students at New York City Community College at how a black Dean of Liberal

Arts and Sciences could live in the post-World War II United States and oppose the establishment of an autonomous black studies department in their college in downtown Brooklyn. I then began an effort at recording recollections from my earliest childhood through my adulthood, in order to answer, for my own edification, the question of how my experiences had brought me as a black to the way I think and feel about matters and events around me. Obviously then, it was not a matter of taking a subject and seeing where it went. Rather, it was looking at a state of mind and trying to see what were its antecedents.

Documentation of some of the basic matters regarding the officers and men of the 1325th Engineer Regiment in which I served is not possible. One reason is that, as the chief of the Army Reference Branch of the National Personnel Records Center in St. Louis told me in August of 1993, "Personnel rosters for the years 1944, 1945, and 1946 were destroyed in accordance with the General Records Schedule." Documenting impressions of this miserable regiment was further complicated by the fact that I could not find any of its members who cared to reflect on their service in it. One, when contacted by telephone, denied that he had ever served in the regiment, preferring to cite the infantry regiment to which he had been transferred as the unit in which he performed his World War II service. Others to whom I wrote at the suggestion of Baynard Hare, my counterpart in Headquarters and Service Company of the 1325th, simply did not reply. As a consequence, the reflections of Baynard Hare, which I cite, my own feelings and those spontaneous, collective, at-the-moment assessments which I recall being made at the time by my fellow conscripts constitute both the reportage of the phenomena and the meat of the corroborative evidence which undergird my recollections as regards the 1325th Engineer General Service Regiment.

The lack of documentation of other events is by reason of the fact that some evidence or information has been lost forever. For example, on April 12, 1970, I gave a talk entitled "Black Personality Disorders: The Legacy of White Racism" at the Unitarian Fellowship here in Rockland County. This was announced in the April 11, 1970, issue of the *Rockland Journal-News*, a Rockland County newspaper. It was probably the most intriguing presentation I have made, but it is not possible to re-create it. Coming as it did in a period when I was deep in my study of the condition of black men, it was, no doubt, based on considerable research. I had read Frantz Fanon's *The Wretched of the Earth* (1963), the English translation of his *Toward the African Revolution* (1967), and possibly David Caute's *Frantz Fanon* (1970). I undoubtedly read Peter Geismar's *Fanon* (1971) after this speech. Whatever I said to the Unitarians on that April Sunday in 1970 was probably colored by thinking expressed by or attributed to Frantz Fanon, the revolutionary black Martinican psychiatrist to whose age cohort of blacks, born in 1925, I belong. However, I cannot remember a single thing that I said and can find neither the manuscript of the talk nor notes which I may have used for the presentation.

On the other hand, my recollections and impressions regarding the events at both New York City Technical College and Bergen Community College are relatively fresh, documentable and possible of comparison and assessment against the countervailing recollections and viewpoints of highly literate and articulate people who remain at the ready to cross swords with those holding other viewpoints. Some of these people, however, are at a disadvantage in this arena because they cannot interrupt and shout down a memoir. They must take the trouble to read, to think and to formulate their rebuttals.

Readers are on notice that this book is a memoir and is "as recalled by Harry B. Dunbar," in some instances fifty years after the fact and often unaided by any primary documentation. Readers are reminded, however, that I have followed a principle which I learned from Dr. William Brickman, my historiography teacher at New York University, who taught us that "when the sources are silent the wise do not speak." I speak on things for which my memory is the primary source. Faulty though it may be, that is most often a source which can be checked against the recollections of others who were witnesses to the same events. Dizzy Dean, that eminent philosopher, once said, "It ain't braggin' if you really done it." I paraphrase him here by saying, "It really happened because I was there and I remember it." Or more accurately, this memoir reports what I remember and the way I remember it. A case in point: One of my three sisters commented that my characterization of another sister is not quite accurate. However, I have not changed that characterization because that is the way I see her. So it is throughout this book.

Acknowledgments

I am indebted to several persons whose support, encouragement, advice and expertise were given without measure. My wife Charlene, since our marriage, has been beside me in my every endeavor throughout my career and has been a tower of strength when the chips were down. Without her loyal and faithful collaboration I would not have gotten to this point in my life and career. She read a purported first draft of the manuscript and pointed out errors and one looming, egregious omission which would have been unforgivable.

I am grateful to Louise Robbins for reading the manuscript many times (once on an airplane traveling to and from England) and making corrections of style, grammar, context, tense, and voice and for offering suggestions which have yielded a more coherent and readable book.

I am very appreciative to my sisters Catherine, Louise, and Ida for taking time during our annual family Christmas gathering to reminisce with me about our childhood to help me sharpen my recollection of some events and people from the tumultuous days in the years that we lived as children in the infamous Hudson, New York. My brother Henry, unfortunately, could not contribute to this, since he was too young to remember any of it.

I, better than most, can appreciate the sacrifices made by Hobart Jarrett and William E. Nelson, Jr. to read, comment on and make suggestions to me for the improvement of the manuscript for this book. Both of these men had manuscripts of their own in advanced stages, but made hiatuses in their momentums to read mine, effectively giving my work time which they can never retrieve. I am grateful to them.

Daphne Estwick inconvenienced herself to review this manuscript at a time when she could have declined with my full understanding. I know something about the workload of academic administrators with the kinds of responsibilities she has. It is for that reason that I am deeply grateful to her for the insightful critique she made of the manuscript for this book.

Nathan Wright, Jr. generously read the manuscript (on an airplane traveling to and from France), commented on it, and telephoned me at least twice with encouragement. His insights on the influence of the communities where I lived on my development are on the mark. The fraternal bond that exists between me and him, and between William Nelson and me, despite my philosophical differences with both of them on matters of strategy for the liberation of blacks, transcends those differences. I am a better person for the bond that exists between us.

Finally, Paul Robeson, Jr. was encouraging and gracious in telephoning me to inform me orally of his forthcoming written permission to quote from one of his works and to personally encourage my effort.

Harry B. Dunbar
West Nyack, N.Y.
December 19, 1994

CHAPTER 1

By Their Fruit You Shall Know Them

On reflection, the years between 1925 and 1943 were halcyon years in my life for it was in those years that the foundation was laid for what has been a very satisfying adulthood. I was born on Mother's Day, Sunday, May 10, 1925, in Mineola on New York's Long Island, to parents who were natives of Jamaica in the West Indies and who were surely the most significant influence on my formative years.

My Father

My father, Shafter Nathan Dunbar, a minister in the African Methodist Episcopal (A.M.E.) Zion Church, was a remarkable man. Born in 1887 in Helicon, a rural community in the mountains of the Parish of St. Ann, he was a member of the generation of Marcus Garvey, a personality with whom he had much in common. S. N. Dunbar was born of humble parents, who, from what I have been able to determine, made their living from the land. He was a very private person. I never heard him say, even once, that he had a difficult life growing up in a poor family. In fact, I never heard him discuss his family at all. It was from my mother that I learned much of what I know about him, including the fact that he was a Baptist when she met him in Jamaica. While I do not know much about his life as a youth, from my own observation of his home in Jamaica I can easily conclude that it was the hard life common to poor agrarian people living on marginal land. Life there has changed little today from what I have observed.

My father had three brothers and a sister, none of whom I ever met. I believe that one of his brothers had already left Jamaica to live in Cuba by the time he took us to Jamaica to visit in 1930. I never knew my paternal grandfather, but as a five-year-old I did meet my paternal grandmother when my father took all of us, that is, my mother, my sisters Catherine, Louise, and Ida and me, to Jamaica to visit his aging mother and other relatives. (My brother Henry had not yet been born.) My recollections of my paternal grandmother are only that she was very old, could not see and sat in a chair all day, eating peppermint candy.

While there is no record of what motivated him to do so, I suspect that because of the lack of opportunities in Jamaica, my father migrated to Cuba and, according to papers I have seen among his belongings, worked there as a laborer for the United Fruit Company. I am unable to date his departure from Jamaica, so I do not know how long he lived in Cuba, although I know that he arrived in New York

By Their Fruit You Shall Know Them ∞ 3

in 1916. In any event, he stayed in Cuba long enough to learn Spanish. I know this because when we were children he began to teach us Spanish. I can still remember the workbooks with drill exercises in them from which he had us do written homework. I can also remember his dissatisfaction with my progress in the lessons he was giving and his banishing me from them. Only at my mother's intervention did I get back into his course.

When my father came to New York in 1916, he lived in Harlem at 208 West 134th Street and held a job downtown in the Waldorf Astoria Hotel. I do not know what he did there, though I know he began work on June 19, 1917.

Some time around this period he began preaching on the streets of Harlem. I learned this because in going through his papers I found his license to preach on the streets of New York. It seems that in the era of the 1920s one had to have a license from the City of New York to speak or preach on the street. My father's license, called an exhorter's license, authorized him to hold forth on 129th Street.

Somehow, and I am not sure how, my father attracted the attention of one of the A.M.E. Zion bishops. It might have been Bishop Lee, or Bishop Clement, or Bishop Caldwell or Bishop Kyles. I do recall that Bishop Kyles was a guest in our home once. In any event, the 129th Street Exhorter soon came into an assignment as an assistant to the pastor of Mother A.M.E. Zion Church on 137th Street.

I have often wondered recently if my father went out on the streets of Harlem to hear another exhorter from St. Ann's Bay, Jamaica, who was encouraging blacks in Harlem to join him in a return to Africa. While I never discussed this with my father, nor did I ever hear him say so, I have concluded that he did indeed listen to Marcus Garvey on the street and that he accepted much of what Garvey said. While he was opposed to some of the projects that Garvey espoused, particularly the Black Star Line and the return to Africa project, S. N. Dunbar was a great supporter of his pride-in-the-black-race concept.

Anyone who knew my father recalls that he was well ahead of his time in referring to us as black men and women. As far back as I can remember he used this term in referring to our race. My recollections of his comments on this subject go back at least twenty-five years before it became fashionable in the late 1960s to refer to us as blacks. I am sure that his use of the term predates my recollections. I suspect that my father's use of the term was related to his agreement with Marcus Garvey on the whole matter of race pride, and his further agreement that the term "black" was not in itself derogatory to us, but represented rather accurately our racial identity, and taken outside of the pejorative connotation that others put on the term, the term "black" was most appropriate in referring to us. I believe that my father saw Marcus Garvey as a significant articulator of the longings and aspirations of black people.

Some time after World War I, my father became a minister assigned to his own church in the New York Conference of the African Methodist Episcopal Zion Church. He then held appointments in his own right to small churches on eastern Long Island. Somewhere around 1921 or 1922 he was appointed pastor of the A.M.E. Zion Church in Westbury, Long Island. It was while pastoring there that he sent to Jamaica for Elma Russell-Brown, whom he married, and began his role as husband and

By Their Fruit You Shall Know Them ∞ 5

father, as well as his fifty-year career of pastoring churches in New York State, ranging from Long Island to as far upstate as Hudson, New York. During his pastorate in Westbury a new edifice was built. That building still serves the congregation there today. He then pastored churches in Hempstead, Port Chester, Hudson, Middletown and Sparkill. Over the course of his pastorate, he became an excellent preacher. His sermons, nearly always built on biblical texts, were demonstrations of his mastery of extemporaneous presentation and were always replete with quotations from scripture and from secular literature, which he quoted at will, from memory.

My father cherished books and his library was substantial. He had a full set of the works of Dickens, a collection on the history of the Roman Empire, a set of encyclopedias, a collection of Bible commentaries, and the voluminous reference works which clergymen use in preparing their sermons. He was a voracious reader and was well informed on current affairs. I am convinced that his scholarly bent was a subliminal influence on me. My own scholarly interests and habits were spawned and nurtured by his example. I can pinpoint his example as the locus of inspiration for my very first research effort.

As a senior in Tappan Zee High School I had as a teacher a Miss Mary Brightbill, who told us that no matter what it was that we planned to do after graduation from high school, we should try to learn as much as we could about some subject which interested us and we should do that by starting to read everything we could find on that subject. While I have neither the slightest recollection of how I picked my subject nor any memory of how my interest turned to it, I do recall that I went through a period when my interests were in the direction of abstractions or ideas and that I was very interested in reading papers and tracts which came out of the noncredit division of Columbia University. In any case, in response to Miss Brightbill's admonition, I decided to learn all I could about Emperor Maximilian of Mexico. My further recollection is that I did all of the research in my father's library. I handed the paper in to my history teacher, Mr. Dixon, but I believe that such papers had to pass muster with Miss Brightbill as well. My point here is that my father's library was a rich treasury for study in certain areas of history and literature. I can honestly say that his studious example, the great library resource which he had in our home and the "guidance counseling" of my mother, which led me into a purely academic curriculum, formed the basis for any scholarly habits which I developed and for my general disposition to the life of the mind.

An anecdote related by my mother about my father and his books comes to mind here. As I have indicated, my family moved a good deal during my childhood. Packing up the household belongings for the mover was a big undertaking. Making the library ready for the moves was a major task to which my father gave his full attention. He developed a system of tying the books with heavy cord in bundles measuring about two feet in height. It took a great many bundles to accommodate all of the books, but my father went to great lengths to be certain that all were securely bundled and loaded into the van. My mother once made the observation that she didn't think that he would miss any one of the five of his children if that child did not make it to the railroad or bus station for the move, but that he made sure that every book was taken care of. His response was that he was sure that we would find our way on our own, but that the books could not.

My father was a very conservative man on most issues. For example, in labor disputes he always took the side of management. I never heard him take the part of the strikers. His constant comment was, "The unions are ruining this country." He seemed to believe that one ought to work in order to deserve to eat. To my mind this would explain his oft-expressed disdain for able-bodied men who could be seen idle day after day and then be seen in the evening, to use his term, "picking their teeth." He seemed to feel that a meal was a reward for a day's work. Politically, my father was also very conservative. Though he was never enrolled in a political party, as far as I know, and never seemed to favor one over the other, he was an inveterate supporter of incumbents. He always said of challengers, "They wouldn't do any better if they were in there."

Mother

My mother, née Elma Alexandria Russell-Brown, was a remarkable person. As social classes go in Jamaica, she enjoyed higher status than did my father, whom she met as a young woman when she went to Falmouth, in the Parish of Trelawny, to work in a store. It was then, while visiting her sister Isabel who was teaching in the nearby community of Helicon, where my father was born and lived, that Mother met Daddy. Coming from urban St. Andrew Parish (Kingston) she was a member of a civil service family. Her father was the lighthouse keeper at

Negril, at the opposite end of the island from her native Kingston. (Before she died, she took us to visit the lighthouse, which still stands.) I never knew her parents, but did know two of her sisters. One, Isabel, came to the United States several times, and we got to know her rather well. The other, whom we called M.D., we knew less well.

My mother, an immigrant from Jamaica, arrived in the United States in 1922. She taught herself what the five of her children were learning in school by reading the books which we brought home. In addition, she read almost as widely as did my father. Moreover, she talked to members of the congregations in my father's churches who were knowledgeable about American curricula, schools and courses. She would talk with me about these things and advise me. I attribute to her the motivation to pursue the course of study which resulted in my earning the high-quality secondary school diploma which I have on the bookcase in my home office. I am very proud of this diploma, awarded by the University of the State of New York Education Department, duly signed by the associate commissioner of education, bearing the raised seal of the University of the State of New York and numbered 227383 in the June 1942 series. This diploma lets it be known that Harry B. Dunbar, "having satisfactorily passed examinations in English four years, French three years, intermediate algebra, plane geometry and American history and having submitted evidence of the satisfactory completion of an approved four-year course in the Tappan Zee High School is entitled to this College Entrance Diploma."

The documentation of the rigor of the studies represented by this diploma, which can be tracked by number in the archives at Albany, is very meaningful to me. What makes me most proud of it, though, is the fact that my mother was my "guidance counselor" and was the source of the counseling which resulted in this achievement. Mother was the person to whom the five of us turned for all of our needs. My father was the final arbiter of major matters. He rarely interposed judgments in matters in which Mother had given us consent or advice. Mother devoted herself to homemaking and to the welfare of our father and the five of us. In his own way my father devoted himself to her and to the work of his church and his congregation. I believe that I inherited from him a sense of commitment to my work which arose from his example. From Mother I believe that I inherited a disposition for observing from a position in the background.

My Siblings

My three sisters and my brother were an integral part of my childhood. I am the eldest. Catherine is a year younger than I. Louise is two years younger than I; Ida is three years younger than I; and Henry, the youngest, is five years younger than I. Each of us is his own person. However, I think I see the marks of both of my parents in each. It is my own feeling that together we constitute an illustration of the saying that the fruit does not fall far from the tree.

Catherine has a remarkable memory for our late father's remarks, ideas and lessons from the family setting. One story she relates exemplifies his quick wit. As she recalls it, one Saturday night when we were children he was polishing our shoes, as he frequently did. He had an open bottle of liquid shoe polish on the kitchen floor as he worked. He forbade us to pass through the kitchen because, as he put it, "Someone is going to knock over the shoe polish." A moment later, with none of us in the kitchen, he knocked over the polish. His prompt riposte was, "I told you someone was going to knock over that polish."

After graduating from Tappan Zee High School, Catherine went to work in the administrative offices of the Schenley Distilling Company and then in the national office of the United Electrical, Radio and Machine Workers of America, both in New York City. She matriculated at Hunter College and attended at night, while working for the union in the daytime. She earned a bachelor's degree and a master's degree in business education. She made a career teaching typewriting in New York City junior and senior high schools. She retired in 1981 and joined the adjunct faculty of Rockland Community College, where she taught English as a second language.

Louise has the temperament of our mother, which probably explains Mother's decision to stay in Louise's home after our father died and she sold their home and began to spend time with us and in Jamaica in the winter. Louise has an ear for the Jamaican accent and the ability to decode the argot. I can still remember her recounting the story of her standing with a crowd waiting for the supermarket in Discovery Bay to reopen at 2 P.M. as announced. It seems that when the proprietor returned, the indignant patrons who had been waiting in the hot sun admonished him that "two long gone." Louise knew that the translation of this was, "It is long past two o'clock."

Louise attended Hunter College, earning a bachelor's degree in English and a master's degree in administration.

She taught in junior high schools in New York City and earned a doctor of education degree from Hofstra University. She began her career in higher education teaching remedial reading at Queens College of the City University of New York (CUNY) and later at Suffolk County Community College before moving to Hofstra University's New Opportunities at Hofstra (NOAH) program.

Ida fell closer to the tree than any other of the fruit of the S. N. Dunbar family tree. She is more nearly our mother than either of the other daughters. She has an affinity for Jamaica and things Jamaican. She can understand Jamaican dialect and idiom, spoken by natives at conversational speed. She can speak it with near-native skill and does so most often without being detected as a foreigner by natives. A Jamaican woman said of her several years ago, "Miss Ida is Jamaican you know." Ida was Mother's companion in Jamaica in the latter years of Mother's life when we had reservations about her being there by herself. Ida spent all of her summers there with Mother, and she continues to do so today, even after Mother's death. Ida is more like Mother than her sisters are. She is more like Mother than Henry or I are like our father.

Ida earned a bachelor's degree in business from the City College of New York and a master's degree in counseling. She made a career as a counselor and assistant principal in high schools in New York City, notably Boys' and Girls' High School and Midwood High School, before retiring in 1985.

Henry, with his sharp ear for linguistic inflection, can reproduce with uncanny accuracy our late father's Jamaican-accented English. One such example comes easily to memory. In the 1960s the five of us were rediscovering Jamaica. As all returning travelers do, we related to friends and family the wonders which we had seen on the beautiful "island in the sun." Henry's re-creation of Daddy's "I born there, you know" is a classic in its own right when taken in the context of Daddy's position that nothing had changed in Jamaica from the time he left there, probably in the first decade of the twentieth century, to the 1960s when he was hearing these romanticized tales from returning tourists. As he used to say repeatedly, "When you touch Jamaica, you touch trouble."

Henry earned a bachelor's degree from New York University and a doctor of dental surgery degree from the School of Dentistry of Howard University. He then served for four years as a captain in the U.S. Army Dental Corps, mainly in Japan. After military service he set up a dental practice in the borough of Queens in New York City. After several years of practice there he moved to Long Island, first into a medical center in Wyandanch in which he was a partner with several physicians, then into an office in Hempstead as a sole practitioner.

Me

By reason of my father's occupation as a minister in the New York Conference of the A.M.E. Zion Church, which appoints ministers to churches on one-year assignments, as a youth I lived in and attended the public schools in many communities in New York State, including Westbury and Hempstead on Long Island, Port Chester in Westchester

County, Hudson in Columbia County, Middletown in Orange County, and finally Sparkill in Rockland County. Each of these communities had a small black population, schools that were integrated and harmonious relations between the races and ethnic groups living in them. I do recall, however, that blacks were not treated very sensitively in the textbooks that we used and that at least twice in my elementary school experience there were days when I did not want to go to school because Africa and blacks were to be the topics of the lessons on the days involved. I have since come to associate my teachers' attitudes with the observation of Sterling Stuckey that leading scholars in distinguished graduate schools such as Harvard and Columbia were teaching their students that Africans had always "groped in barbarism and never originated a regular organization among themselves." Some of my teachers were trained at Columbia University by disciples of John W. Burgess, who argued that "a black skin means membership in a race of men . . . which has never created any civilization of any kind."

On the whole I would say, though, that race per se was not a particularly intrusive matter in my early childhood and adolescence. My classmates were predominantly white, my playmates were primarily black. As an adult, I do not have any friendships which go back to my elementary school days, since I did not attend any school for more than three years and moved away from the communities where I had attended school.

I have some fairly clear recollections from the three years that we lived in Hudson, New York. I was ten years of age and in the fifth grade when we moved there from Port Chester, New York, in 1935. My report card for that year, the only year for which I have such a record, shows that I attended the Williams School for Grades 5 and 6, received good grades in almost all of the subjects I took during the 1935–1936 school year, and did poorly only in arithmetic. In looking at the name "K. A. Best," under the date of June 19, 1936, on the Certificate of Promotion section of this report card, I note that I was promoted to Grade 6A at the Williams School. From this I am able to recall "K. A. Best" as Mrs. Katherine Best, who was my teacher in Grade 6B and also the wife of the district attorney of Columbia County. I remember the subject having come up during a current events discussion in class, probably during the 1936–1937 school year when I was in the sixth grade.

In the 1937–1938 school year I was in the seventh grade and a student at Hudson Junior High School. For that school year I can remember only that my parents let me join the Hudson Boys Club and that I went there after school and played pool, among other things.

The 1938–1939 school year saw me in the eighth grade at Hudson Junior High, where I evidently did well academically. I have, among the records which my mother gave me, a card designating me as a Hudson Junior High School honor student for the third quarter of 1938. The signature of William Goff, an official of the Star Theatre, under the date of May 11, 1938, on the back of the card helps me to remember that one of the perks which honor students received was free admission to the Star upon showing this card. On the day after my birthday in 1938 I exercised this privilege.

Hudson was a bawdy city in the 1930s. Columbia Street, the street on which we lived, was a notorious street and the center of the city's red-light district. Teenager that I was in 1938, I did not know this, but learned of it some fifty-five years later from reading an article about Hudson's "Red-Light Past" in the October 21, 1994, issue of the *New York Times*. The reading of this article unleashed a flood of memories heretofore unrecalled.

Two pictures accompany the article. The topmost picture shows six homes alongside each other. The two homes in the foreground triggered a flash of recognition in my memory. The leftmost of these two homes is pictured with Stephen Durham, its owner, on a ladder working on the roof of its porch. The article says that the house is on Columbia Street and was purchased by Durham in 1972 from Mae Gordon, an alleged former madam. I believe that this house is 215 Columbia Street and is the house in which we lived from 1935 to 1938! My belief is reinforced by a visible corridor, which we called "the gangway," and which served as a passageway, between our house and the house next door, giving us access to Columbia Street from our backyard. My belief that this is the house in which we lived is further reinforced by the striking similarity of the house on the other side of the gangway in the picture to that which I remember being there when I lived at 215 Columbia Street. The front entry door and the first- and second-floor windows all fit my recollection.

That house was home to about five black men, who, I believe, worked in either the cement plant or the brickyard, where very many of the black male Hudson residents worked. I remember a woman houseguest of these men who came for frequent and extended visits. I remember something else about those men and that house, something that I saw there, the likes of which I had not seen in my twelve or thirteen years of life in 1937 or 1938, nor in the fifty-six or fifty-seven years since: one day I was in the gangway and looked in the gangway-side window of the house next door, which opened on a bedroom, and beheld the woman houseguest copulating with one of her hosts.

I have recollections of walking down to the Hudson River to see the Dayliner come in. In those days there was a fleet of paddle wheel vessels, called the Hudson River Day Line, which plied the river daily, most often loaded with tourists, and made regular excursion runs from New York City to Albany and back, making stops at various cities, Hudson being one of them. Hudson boys who were strong swimmers used to dive from the pier at Hudson to retrieve coins thrown from the vessels by the passengers. I remember too that the river froze solid in the winter, permitting trucks to be driven across it. Further, I remember that in winter, snow was plowed to the center of Warren Street, the main thoroughfare through the business center of the city of Hudson. In midwinter, when I walked on one side of Warren Street, I could not see people walking on the other side of the street. The wall of snow must have been at least five feet high.

One fall day in 1937 I had a personal traumatic encounter. I was walking back to Hudson Junior High from having lunch at home, when I heard someone call out what I thought was my name. I turned to see who it was, and took a blow in my right eye from a chestnut that was propelled by a slingshot in the hands of a young school dropout, whose name I remember to this day, who was standing on the steps of a building taking random shots at passersby. When I arrived at school, the teacher saw the condition of my eye and had me taken to the hospital. The vision in my right eye was and is substantially impaired from the trauma.

A saloon was located directly across the street from our home on Columbia Street. It was patronized by white people, largely middle European types. Considerable heavy drinking took place in there. The establishment catered to a large takeout clientele who would come with their pitchers and leave with beer by the pitcherful. There was considerable carousing and noisemaking in the place. On New Year's Eve of 1938, a near tragedy for my mother emanated from there.

On the New Year's Eve in question I had gone with my father to the Watch Night Service he was conducting at the church, as he did every New Year's Eve. Some time after midnight, a man came into the service with a message for my father to the effect that my mother had been shot. My father was incredulous, insisting that this could not be, since his wife was at home with their children who were not at the service. He concluded the service and we returned home, to find that mother had indeed been shot. Some drunken patrons from the saloon, including the owner, whom we knew, had come out into Columbia Street just before midnight to take turns firing a shotgun into the air to celebrate the New Year. Mother looked out a second-floor window to see what was going on. One of the revelers, whom she was able to identify by name, took his turn and, with insufficient elevation, fired into the bedroom where my sisters were asleep, and struck Mother in the face with a volley of buckshot pellets. Doctors removed buckshot from Mother's face over ensuing years. Nevertheless, I believe she went to her grave in 1983 with some pellets still in her.

The following June, at the termination of his appointment, my father was transferred to the church at Middletown. I don't know it for a fact, but I believe this may have been the only time in his long career in the ministry that my father made any appeal to the presiding bishop regarding his assignment. I believe he had asked to be moved from Hudson.

From an academic standpoint, my stay in Hudson was a rewarding one. At the end of the 1937–1938 school year, as we were preparing to move to Middletown, New York, I was awarded a certificate known as a Preliminary Certificate, issued by the University of the State of New York, the State Education Department. It certifies that I had "satisfactorily completed the requirements for admission to academic grade in the following subjects at Hudson: Reading, Writing, Spelling, Elementary English, Arithmetic, Geography, Elementary U.S. History." Numbered 3849, dated June 1938 and signed by the associate commissioner and the superintendent of schools in Hudson, this was certification that I was on the Regents track, the college-preparation track in New York State. With this certificate in hand, my transfer to the Regents Diploma track at Middletown High School in September 1938 was seamless.

In looking back at my distant childhood, from the perspective of the senior citizen that I now am, with an eye to assessing that childhood from its black (or Negro) context, I find it relatively unremarkable. In all of our school careers the five of us attended schools where we were in a minority from a racial and an ethnic standpoint. White students of many ethnic strains populated the schools we attended. While there was a scattering of blacks in all of the schools in which we were enrolled, I do not recall any other fellow students who were of Jamaican parents. Further, in nearly all of the courses which I took in the college-preparatory curriculum which I followed in the two high schools I attended, I was often the only black. I do not remember undergoing any undue hectoring because I was black. Nor do I remember any of us having encountered any of the taunts from American blacks of which other blacks of West Indian heritage frequently complain. I can recall only one instance where my race constituted a problem as regards activities in which I participated.

When I moved to Sparkill, I was a junior in high school. In extracurricular activities in Middletown I had been a member of a Boy Scout troop. One of the civics teachers at the high school was the scoutmaster, as well as my academic adviser at school. A Second Class Scout, I was the only black in the troop. After coming to Sparkill I sought to continue my affiliation with scouting and was invited to join the troop in Piermont, which was sponsored by the local Knights of Columbus. The scoutmaster was Mr. Anthony Barone, one of the teachers at Tappan Zee High School, later to become its principal. I had amassed the maximum number of merit badges which a Second Class Scout could accumulate. I had to be a First Class Scout in order to be eligible to pursue more merit badges.

To be a First Class Scout I had to know how to swim. The place where most of the scouts in this area learned to swim was the Nyack YMCA. The problem was that the Nyack YMCA did not allow blacks to use its facilities in 1941.

The long and the short of it was that Mr. Barone made arrangements with the YMCA to permit me to go there when it was closed and to have one of the staff members teach me to swim. I went to take my first lesson. The instructor stood on the edge of the pool and told me what to do. I was not able to follow his instructions. I might have been better able to handle it if he had gotten into the water and demonstrated, but he did not do so. When the lesson ended, I left and never went back. I dropped out of scouting. I could handle the indignity of having to go to the YMCA when it was closed to learn how to swim, because it was a way to reach an objective which I had set for myself. I could not deal with the knowledge that the swim instructor would not get into the water with me to teach me, because I was black.

My elementary and secondary educations were particularly good and have served me well. First, I received a classic academic secondary education without missing a step, so to speak, though I made an odyssey through the schools of the state of New York in obtaining it. I believe that this is attributable to the fact that in New York State the curriculum was fairly well standardized, particularly for students who aspired to the New York State Regents Diploma, as I had.

In December of 1941, in the first semester of my senior year at Tappan Zee High School, the Japanese bombed Pearl Harbor, drawing the United States into war. The

Selective Service System which was already in place was conscripting men from eighteen years of age for military service and putting them through training, ostensibly for a year. However, I cannot recall any who were trained and returned home before the United States joined in the hostilities. In any event, once the United States went to war, the commitment of those drafted changed immediately from one year of service to "the duration plus six months." Thus, to the inevitability of military service for able-bodied men was added an extension of the obligation to cover whatever period the war took, plus six months. Exemptions from military service were not easily come by. Employment in special occupations which were in the interest of the nation was cause for exemption. Attending college was not, as was to be the case later when the United States got into the armed conflict in Korea.

Young men finishing high school had to postpone career plans. To enroll in college was to waste money, because when "your number came up" you had to go, no matter what you were doing. The call-ups intensified. It became a matter of watching your slightly older peers leave and marking time until your number came up. Many young men volunteered rather than wait for the inevitable. I chose to work in order to begin to accumulate a nest egg.

During the summers of 1941 and 1942 I worked on Handwerg's farm, then one of the largest growers of tomatoes in New York State. I picked tomatoes and corn. I also worked for a friend who had a small lawn-tending business with a few clients he had "inherited" from his older brothers. In 1943, when he responded to the draft, I served those clients.

At the end of the summer of 1942, I went to work in the machine room of the Robert Gair Company in Piermont, New York. This plant was one of the largest makers of paperboard in the nation. Working as a laborer in the machine room of a paper mill is some of the hardest physical labor there is. There is no respite as the machine churns out tons of paperboard per hour. For days one labors under the illusion that tending the dry end of a papermaking machine "piling down" tons of paperboard per shift is the most physically taxing occupation. However, when the siren goes off announcing a breakdown, and all hands, you included, run, screaming profanities, to take their preassigned positions to do their bit to restore production, you are disabused of the illusion that you had entertained about what hard work is. When you take your position in the pit directly under the hot, relentlessly churning two- or three-ton steel drums to help get out the paper that is choking the mill, then you know what hard work is. Working in the machine room of that paper mill was the most effective motivator I experienced in my working life. It motivated me to prepare myself for more intellectually rewarding and less physically demanding work.

Some time in 1943 I decided that it was time to find less physically stressful work. I started making the rounds of employment agencies in New York City and landed a job in the mail room of the United Electrical Radio and Machine Workers of America (UERMWA), an affiliate of the Congress of Industrial Organizations (CIO). I never knew what my father thought of my making common cause with those who were in his opinion wantonly "ruining this country." He never commented to me on the subject. As I reflect on it today, I realize that in his view I was helping to facilitate their mischief with the mass mailings of the newspapers, tear sheets and the like that I bundled, weighed, affixed postage to and took to the post office for dispatch to UERMWA locals all over the nation. I remained at UE, as we used to refer to it, until I received my "greeting" from the draft board in Pearl River.

CHAPTER 2

Under the Colors

Uncle Sam and Racial Reality

The years 1944 through 1946 were the years that opened to me the experience of an ever-wider social and geographic world. In May of 1943 when I turned eighteen, I registered for the military draft as was required by law. I was inducted into the army on January 14, 1944, and was called to active duty on February 4, 1944. I was sent to the U.S. Army Reception Center at Camp Upton on Long Island, where I was processed, along with other black draftees, and then shipped to Camp Claiborne, Louisiana. There I was assigned to the 1325th Engineer General Service Regiment, a black labor battalion which was being activated.

The U.S. Army was the venue for my first experience with enforced racial segregation. Before that February morning in 1944 when I arrived at Camp Upton I had never been forced into a racially segregated situation. Even in the situation which I recounted earlier regarding my attempt to learn to swim at the Nyack YMCA, I had chosen to participate in that segregated activity. At Camp Upton, the U.S. Army ordered me into a group in which all of the men were black, and that condition obtained throughout my entire army experience in Louisiana, New York, France, Belgium, and Guam. Only when I was sent to the Army University Center (AUC) on the island of Oahu in 1945 was I assigned by the army to an integrated group. White and black soldiers were students at the AUC, and the classes and the dormitories were racially integrated. One of my classmates and dormitory mates there was Sam Wanamaker, the actor, who, after demobilization, played on the stage opposite Ingrid Bergman in the play *Joan of Lorraine,* and in movies, before being blacklisted in the 1950s due to allegedly leftist affiliations. I remember him as a very friendly man and was saddened when I read of his blacklisting and of his self-exile in England.

Given my background, the experience of being snatched from the environment in which I had spent my first eighteen years and of being sent to the racially hostile environment of Camp Claiborne, Louisiana, to take basic training in a black labor battalion constituted a grueling rite of passage to adulthood for me.

Life in the army in 1944 represented a major change of environment for most eighteen-year-old men, I am sure. I can tell you that for me, a black eighteen-year-old who had been born and raised in New York State, who had never been away from home before, who had not been anywhere outside of the New York, New Jersey, Connecticut area, and who had never experienced enforced racial segregation before, the adjustment called for was a major one.

The circumstances surrounding my arrival at Camp Claiborne, Louisiana, in late February 1944 are etched sharply in my memory. We had traveled several days by troop train from Camp Upton, New York. Since troop movements constituted top-secret intelligence, neither we nor the enemy had any idea where we were going, though we observed station signs and other indications of place names. One member of our contingent had been a dining car chef in civilian life and had traveled on some of the routing. He was able to give us some information as to where we were. However, with all of the backing into sidings and the circuitous meanderings which the troop train made, he soon became as disoriented as the rest of us. I suppose the members of the cadre who were escorting us to Louisiana knew where we were headed, but they never told us.

We arrived at Claiborne late of an evening. I recall being very hungry and going with the others to the mess hall for dinner. Evidently the feeding for the day was over and we had not been expected. The only thing being served was boiled cabbage, a food that I do not eat. That was the entree. The cabbage was what happened to have been left over after the evening meal had been served to the soldiers already stationed at the base. I went to bed hungry on my first night at Camp Claiborne.

The next day, along with the others assigned to the 1325th Engineers, I was given the inoculations, the orientation, the lectures on military discipline, was issued clothing and equipment, and then began basic training. The experience required major adjustments.

One adjustment was to the types of men who were in the pool of men assigned to the regiment. From what I have since read about the profiles of enlisted men in World War II, I would classify the group in which I found myself as being in the lowest quartile, using any measure you might choose. They were, for the most part, men who had not graduated from high school. Many had never attended, even for a short period of time. The personal standards of language, general deportment, and the like, were astonishing to me. Living at close quarters with them was an education in itself.

The officer corps of this regiment was pretty well what the regiment merited. In general the officers did not measure up, in my mind, to the standards that I had idealized—standards met by even the "ninety-day wonders" who were coming out of Officer Candidate School in those days. In any case, all of the officers of the 1325th Engineer General Service Regiment were white except two. These two were the regimental chaplain, a captain from Oklahoma, and the regimental supply officer, a warrant officer from Atlanta.

The regimental commander, a white colonel, who like many of the other officers in the regiment had been employed in the construction industry in civilian life, seemed to me a caricature of the classic superintendent of prisons in movies. I don't know what made me see him in that light, except possibly the fact that I felt like a condemned man during the entire period of my service in that regiment.

Perhaps one of the most vivid memories that I have of the racist U.S. Army of World War II comes through the prism of my recollection of the power and majesty of that full colonel of the Corps of Engineers who commanded the miserable regiment in which I served. It provides some rationale for my harsh characterization of my commanding officer.

The warrant officer of the regiment (a black man) had done something that the colonel believed merited stern punishment. Obviously the punishment was designed to humiliate as well as to deter him from further malfeasance. The warrant officer was made to dig a "six-by-six" in front of regimental headquarters. In the military, in those days anyway, a "six-by-six" was a hole in the ground, six feet wide, six feet long and six feet deep. The digging of these holes was routine punishment meted out to enlisted men in the 1325th Engineers.

Reporting to my duty station in regimental headquarters that morning and having to pass that black officer digging a hole in front of the colonel's regimental command post was humiliating to me, a humiliation that I still feel when I think about it forty-seven years later. I attribute to the colonel the responsibility for this indignity which he permitted to be visited upon one of the two black officers, the only two officers with whom the men in the regiment could pridefully identify. I am sure that white officers in that regiment were punished for infractions. However, I know of none who, as part of his punishment, was humiliated in the presence of the men he led.

Our Trainers

Our military training was remarkably effective, given the composition of the pool of trainees and the quality of those responsible for our training, the cadre and the officer corps.

The pool of trainees was top-heavy with uneducated, or poorly educated, unmotivated, low-achieving men, largely from the rural South. The term "cadre" was applied to those enlisted men who had been in the army for perhaps a year or more, had been through basic training, and were selected to lead the training of new "enlisted men," "recruits" or "trainees," each of which term was used to describe newly inducted men. The cadre men had absorbed the military training with an aplomb that recommended them as drillmasters for recruits. However, they were men who were of the same profile as the trainees, except that they had been through the training cycle at least once; some seemed to have gone around three times.

The cadre was directed by a group of officers who, to put it charitably, were not in the top half of their classes in Officer Candidate School. Some of them had been officers in other units and had been transferred to the 1325th; others appeared to be in their first assignment after graduating from the U.S. Army Engineer Officer Candidate School at Fort Belvoir, Virginia. There was one exception. Before our regiment was deployed to Europe, the "prison superintendent" colonel was transferred out and command of the regiment was given to a colonel who was reportedly a graduate of the U.S. Military Academy at West Point. He impressed me as a high-caliber soldier and man. I often wondered what it was that he had done to draw the assignment of commanding a regiment like the 1325th Engineer General Service Regiment.

There was a certain amount of cynicism among the troops about the background of some of our officers. I have never forgotten the barracks yarns about the regimental surgeon, a major from Georgia. The barracks sociologists had it that he came from a prominent family with considerable influence in Georgia. So great was their influence that the family had been able to get him a job as a delivery boy in a drug store when he dropped out of high school. Their influence, however, did not cross the threshold of the local draft board. But the boy had great interest in medicine, as these barracks genealogists and biographers told it, and so it was that, unable to keep their son out of the army, the family was able to parlay their influence into getting him commissioned as a major in the U.S Army Medical Corps. However, they could only get him into a black regiment. He was thankful for little things. I am too. I never had occasion to go on sick call during my tour in the army!

Our Training

Once basic training was over, military specialty training began. There were engineer specialty schools at Camp Claiborne, where various members of the several companies were sent to be trained in military occupational specialties such as demolition, Bailey-bridge construction, operation of road graders and the like. Instead of going to a military occupation specialty school, I became the company clerk for Company F and, ultimately, battalion sergeant major for the second battalion. Typewriting, one of the two nonacademic courses which I had taken in high school, positioned me for my military occupational specialty. Middletown High School gave the U.S Army at least one administrative noncommissioned officer.

My duty station was in regimental headquarters, where I reported each day. That is how I had the occasion to be one of those to observe the humiliation of the black warrant officer. My job was to maintain the service records of the men in Company F and to prepare its payroll every month. In addition, I was the administrative noncommissioned officer accountable for the service records of the men in Companies D and E. I reported to the personnel officer, a young lieutenant from Maryland, who was a fairly decent chap. My position as company clerk gave me some perspective on the backgrounds of the enlisted men in the regiment. Unfortunately, I never had access to the personnel records of the officers and thus was unable to verify the reports on the civilian work experience of the regimental surgeon, or of any other officer.

Some time after the regiment had finished its basic and specialty training, the several companies were deployed on strategic maneuvers and bivouacs in the various swamps that abound in Louisiana. These exercises were designed to measure the efficiency of the 1325th Engineers under conditions which approximated those we might encounter in the theater of operations. Ostensibly, high-ranking officers from the army command level came to observe and evaluate our perfomance in the field.

In early June, the invasion of France by the Allied forces led by General Eisenhower took place. About the middle of June the regiment began to grant furloughs to the troops on a wholesale basis. All of the thousand or so of us must have been granted furloughs between the middle of June and the end of August. I came home in time to attend my sister Catherine's graduation from Tappan Zee High School. I do not remember how many days furlough I had, but about four days of it had to be used for travel, because the rail trip took about two days each way. I went to New Orleans and caught the Crescent City Limited to New York. Other than attending Catherine's graduation I can remember only one other thing that I did on that furlough. I went into Harlem to meet another member of my regiment who lived there and with whom I had traveled home. We went to a seedy bar with some girls he knew and drank some of the worst whiskey I have ever tasted. We then went downtown to Pennsylvania Station and caught the train back to Louisiana.

Marking Time

Beginning at about the time I got back to Claiborne after my furlough, I had the feeling that the 1325th was marking time. Various projects were assigned to the several companies. One company would be sent out to build a stretch of road. Another would be ordered to build a bridge over a small stream. The other companies would remain on the post doing military drills or qualifying on the rifle range. (I finally qualified with an M1 rifle, after substantial sustained effort.)

Late that summer I went to a dance in one of the United Service Organizations (USO) clubs on the post. During the dance a disturbance broke out. It ended up in what I considered to be a riot. I fled the club, as did hundreds of others, and made my way back to my barracks. I later learned that the disorder had spread to most of the black areas of the camp and had resulted in considerable destruction of property. To this day I do not know what caused the riot or exactly what happened as it went on. What I do know is that some time that winter, when our regiment was stationed in England, in my capacity as noncommissioned officer in charge of preparing the payroll, I received a directive to deduct 17 cents from the pay of every man who was in the company when we were stationed at Camp Claiborne. This was a penalty for "U.S. Government Property Lost or Damaged." I was told that the riot damage at Camp Claiborne had been assessed and that an equal share was allocated to every enlisted man in every unit that was on that base when the incident took place. The entry "Due US GPLD $ .17" was entered into each soldier's record and 17 cents was deducted from his pay, wherever in the world he happened to be. (Later, when we got to France, I dutifully made the appropriate entries in the records of all of the men in Company F, my own record included.)

We languished in Camp Claiborne, marching at half step so to speak, until September. By then, presumably, the efficiency experts who had observed our performance in the field judged the 1325th Engineer General Service Regiment to be fit to be committed to one of the theaters of operations. The barracks cynics sneered that the white folks were ready to get us out of there, and that in effect we were being condemned to overseas duty because of the destruction we had wrought during the riot at Claiborne. Whichever reason may explain it, the fact is that in September our unit was issued new clothing and equipment.

All of the regimental equipment was crated. All equipment that was to go with us was labeled "TAT" ("To Accompany Troops"). Somewhere in the period between the riot and September, the new West Point colonel took command of the mission-fit regiment and we boarded a troop train and shipped out to what turned out to be Camp Shanks, New York, for deployment to the European theater of operations.

Camp Shanks was not just any embarkation camp but one in Orangeburg, New York, about three miles from where I lived in Sparkill, New York, and had been built on some of the tomato and corn fields that I had worked two years before, as a field hand on Handwerg's farm.

I got the word out that I was in Camp Shanks and one of my neighbors got word to me of a hole in the fence where he would pick me up. He did this every night for the week or so that I was there and brought me back early each morning. I visited home several times during the week or so that I was there. Finally, we were put on a troop train and taken somewhere that I think might have been in New Jersey. We were ferried to Staten Island and went aboard the U.S. Army Transport *Sea Tiger*. My record shows that we departed on October 22, 1944. We zigzagged our way across the Atlantic to Newport, Wales, arriving on November 2, 1944.

Merrie England

In retrospect, the short sojourn of the 1325th Engineer General Service Regiment in the United Kingdom has left me with only three durable recollections. One has to do with the adverse effect of the climate there on me. The second has to do with going on pass in the city of Wolverhampton. The third has to do with the racial segregation which we endured there.

I am not able to date our stay in England precisely. I know that we landed at Newport, Wales, on November 2, 1944. One recollection is that from the time I got to England I had pains in my ankles, knees and elbows. After I left England this discomfort disappeared, never to return. My hazy recollection is that we went by train from Newport to a British military camp near Wolverhampton. Baynard Hare, my fellow company clerk in Headquarters and Service Company (known to us as H&S Company) recalled, in a letter to me forty-seven years later, that "we encamped in a park that was all that was left of Robin Hood's Sherwood Forest in Egginton, Derbyshire."

I have a clear recollection of getting a pass to go into Wolverhampton one evening. Since everything was blacked out as a defense against air raids, we could not see very much. We went from the camp into Wolverhampton on trucks. I was with one of the cooks from Company F, who was from Harlem. It was he who had had some idea of the route our troop train was taking from Camp Upton to Camp Claiborne. I remember well that we were stopped by a policeman for jaywalking and that my buddy gave the policeman some lip, telling him that he was from New York and had crossed busier streets than any in Wolverhampton and had done so from anywhere in the block that he chose. Further, my buddy told the policeman, "You don't have a gun. You can't make me do anything." My buddy was right, because there was no U.S. Army military policeman along with the bobby to remind my buddy and me that we were required to obey the laws of the country in which we found ourselves. We continued on our way.

We went to a pub and sat and talked with some other soldiers and the English men and women there. Most of the people in the pub were drinking bitters. I tasted it but didn't care for it any more than I had the bad whiskey I had had in Harlem the last night of my furlough. We then went back to the motor pool area, boarded a truck and returned to the base.

My third and strongest recollection of England is the bizarre, racist procedure the army used in awarding passes to go into Wolverhampton. Army policy authorized white soldiers to go to town on one night and black soldiers on another. Thus, if the military police saw a black soldier in town on an even date of the month the MP knew that that black soldier was away from his base without permission. The same would be true for white soldiers on odd days of the month.

Life in France

I cannot pinpoint the exact date on which we left England for France because I cannot remember whether we had our Thanksgiving meal in England or in France. What is certain, though, is that by late November or early December, we had decamped from the vicinity of Wolverhampton, moved on to the port of Southampton, boarded the HMS *Sobieski,* a Polish vessel, crossed the English Channel and disembarked at Le Havre, France. It was not long after that

that we were camped at a place called Étain on the Franco-Belgian border, where our mission was to help backstop the Battle of the Bulge. This was one of the most grueling physical experiences I have ever endured. Unlike the demanding physical exertion I had endured in the heat of the machine room at the Robert Gair Company, this experience was a test of our ability to endure cold. My platoon was lodged in a large building which must have been some type of warehouse. It had concrete flooring on which we slept, in full field gear. I don't remember much else about that station, except U.S. Air Force bombers flying high overhead leaving contrails and our unit being on alert, which could have resulted in momentary orders to move forward and engage the enemy. Unlike the alternative I had as a seventeen-year-old at the Robert Gair paper mill, I could not opt out. Baynard Hare of H&S Company, in his letter to me, later recalled that he had heard the sound of large weapon fire and that the building in which they were billeted bore the marks of a siege.

Once we arrived in France, the several companies of the 1325th Engineers were never again stationed together as a regiment, but were deployed in scattered localities. We were not united again until August 1945, when we were assembled in a staging area outside Marseilles preparing for redeployment to the Western Pacific theater of operations. My recollections focus on Company F's whereabouts and activities after our arrival in France in late November or early December 1944. We were quite often bivouacked in fields, the exact locations of which I do not know, and probably never knew. At one point, though, Company F was set up in a *caserne*, a building in Marle-sur-Serre which had been converted into a military billet. It was the most substantial billet that we inhabited before the end of hostilities.

The attempt to reconstruct the events and activities which the 1325th Engineers participated in or witnessed is frustrated by the fact that these events and activities are now fifty years in the past. The problem is compounded by the fact that in World War II the activities of military units were shrouded in secrecy. It appears that except as they are parts of tactical battle groups, it is not possible to write the history of most World War II units. Usable written documents do not exist for them. For example, it is probably not possible to know from any written record, other than the individual service records of the men in the 1325th Engineer General Service Regiment, that they received the Rhineland Campaign Medal with a battle star for their participation in that campaign. There is probably no documentation anywhere, save in the reminiscences of the now-remaining hundreds of aged veterans, of the thousands of prisoners (captured in the Ardennes offensive) whom they guarded, and of the scut work done by this hapless regiment in providing labor for emergency civil engineering projects behind the lines in December of 1944. In 1993 I was astounded to learn from the chief of the Army Reference Branch in St. Louis that "personnel rosters for the years 1944, 1945 and 1946 were destroyed in accordance with the General Records Schedule." The only roster of any kind which relates to the 1325th Engineers which I have been able to find is a copy of a General Order promulgated on July 10, 1945, by the regimental commander. This document listed only those members of Company F who had been awarded the Good Conduct Medal. (I have reproduced a portion of it in the Notes section at the end of the book.)

As spring 1945 came and the push by Allied forces went into the German heartland, the 1325th Engineers did not follow. The regiment remained in France operating water purification systems, building and maintaining POW camps and guarding prisoners of war.

Somehow, while Company F was billeted at Marle-sur-Serre, our company commander learned that I had some command of the rudiments of the French language and called on me to interpret for him in a controversy in the village, over some damage the regiment had done to a French villager's property. From then on I began to engage in conversation with Frenchmen and had gained a pretty fair level of fluency by the time summer had come. I have often thought that that chance designation as an interpreter by our company commander in that little village in the spring of 1945 was the proximate impetus to my career. Ms. Kahleis, my French teacher at Middletown High School, could not have had any idea that I, one of her first-year and second-year French students, was, no more than six years later, going to land in an obscure little village in her native country interpreting her beloved language, and doing so with little more instruction than she had given me. At least she left me in a better position than that in which H. L. Mencken's French teacher left him. Mencken is reported to have said that when he got to France he could not find a single Frenchman to whom he could speak, because he could not find a Frenchman who had had French 101.

Later in the spring of 1945, Germany surrendered. The U.S. Army devised a highly convoluted system of determining the order in which troops would be rotated back to the United States or deployed elsewhere. The 1325th Engineers did not have enough accumulated points for redeployment to the United States. We received orders to move to a staging area near Marseilles for embarkation. We would travel through the Panama Canal on a thirty-seven-day voyage to the Western Pacific theater of operations. We sailed from Marseilles on July 21, 1945, on the USS *Admiral Koontz*. While we were docked at Honolulu the war in Japan ended. We began to hope that once provisions were taken on, orders would change and that the *Admiral Koontz* would set sail for the United States. This was not to be. We sailed on and arrived at Guam, in the Western Pacific theater of operations, on August 27, 1945.

Baynard Hare (my counterpart in H&S Company) in a letter to me in February of 1992 remembered the voyage: "Trays of food ended on the deck, hammocks were full of soldiers in agony, and everywhere was the smell of vomit. It was the most painfully extended time in the service. Sometimes I think it would have been better up front with Patton."

My own recollection of the trip parallels Hare's, except that I was not seasick. I recall mammoth crap games that went on all day and late into the night. I also recall seeing an acquaintance from Spring Valley High School who was on board the vessel with another army unit that was making the trip with us from France to Guam. I passed the time reading *Lady Chatterly's Lover* and studying a U.S. Armed Forces Institute self-study course in advanced algebra. I never did or submitted any of the exercises, and never completed the course.

TDR&R

Assignment to Guam turned out to be almost like having TDR&R (temporary duty, rest and recuperation). As company clerk, I did Morning Reports, the routine daily status reports on personnel, in which the army accounts for all men available for duty, those sick in quarters, and the like. I also prepared the company payroll. I maintained the individual service records of the men in Company F. Hare recalls duty on Guam as follows:

> Guam was like being sent to summer camp by chastizing parents. France was cold, and the ground was hard. Guam was warm and bright. We spent many hours swimming, going to the movies at the amphitheatre, and even time for reading. The only threatening detail I saw was one in which enlisted men guarded Japanese POWs. Some enterprising guards sold crafts made by these prisoners to other soldiers.

Some time after we had been on Guam for a few months, the army began to offer opportunities for us to go to Hawaii and other places in the Pacific for TDR&R. We were also offered the opportunity to go to the Army University in Hawaii. I applied for admission and was accepted. The trip from Guam to Honolulu was the occasion of my first trip by air. The flight was made on a C-47, with two rows of seats facing each other along the length of the aircraft. Our backs were to the bulkhead. I recall well the fuel stop which the plane made at Johnson Island. The only things on Johnson Island were an airstrip which went from one end of the island to the other, the airplane fuel tanks and the Quonset huts in which the soldiers who serviced the planes lived. I recall very well how the plane touched down at one end of the island and came to a quivering halt at the end of the airstrip, which was at the other end of the island. That was my initiation into air travel.

Return to Sanity

The Army University experience was a satisfying one for me. It was the only racially integrated setting that I experienced in the army. Every other environment to which I was assigned in the military, from the reception center at Camp Upton, New York, to the casual company to which I was assigned to travel to Camp Claiborne, Louisiana, for basic training, to the 1325th Engineers, to the casual company to which I was assigned in Honolulu to travel to Fort Dix, New Jersey, for discharge, was racially segregated. Most of the students at the Army University at Schofield Barracks were white. All of the instructors were white. I took courses in English composition and in German. I received grades of A in the four courses I took and was later able to transfer the credits to New York University.

One of my instructors in English composition at the Army University, a Captain Hart, whose first name I cannot recall, was later to be a colleague of mine at Nathaniel

Hawthorne Junior High School in New York City when I went there to teach in 1954. Some time in the spring of 1946, after the semester had ended, it was determined that I would not have to return to my regiment at Guam but would go to a Replacement Depot in Honolulu, where "orders were cut," as the term went, for me to report to Fort Dix, New Jersey, for separation from the service.

CHAPTER 3

Apprenticeship to the Life of the Mind

Reentry

In the spring of 1946, I was separated from the army at Fort Dix, New Jersey, and returned home to Sparkill to begin the readjustment to civilian life. While at the Army University on Oahu I had decided that I would go to New York University (NYU) instead of Columbia University, which I had considered before being drafted into the army. I applied and was admitted to NYU before returning to the United States. I received credit for the courses I had taken at the Army University, and in the fall of 1946 I began study as a full-time student at New York University under the benefits of the G.I. Bill of Rights.

It would not be an understatement to say that to the same degree that my military service had opened another world to me as a nineteen-year-old, my college experience opened another to me as a twenty-one-year-old. First of all, returning to civilian life as a college student provided a logical venue for me to rejoin my social and intellectual peers, from whom the army had isolated me by placing me in the devastating milieu of a labor battalion. I now realize that I made not one single friend in the army, nor have I kept up with a single person that I met in the 1325th Engineer Regiment. I am convinced that this is a result of the fact that I was thrown into a group that was totally alien to me in outlook, experience, and, for the most part, age. In moments of retrospection I have attempted to reconstruct my social-philosophical state of mind when I returned to the United States in 1946 and began the readjustment to civilian life. What were my feelings on the question of race after the experiences I had undergone in the 1325th Engineers? I felt that race alone was and is an unsuitable criterion on which relationships between people can be satisfactorily based. What had my military experience contributed to or subtracted from me as a person? I learned to be self-reliant even in a group of men all of whom were black. What was I going to try to make of my life? I would now try to make a satisfying life as a cultured man given to thought.

I was relatively well disciplined at age twenty-one, following my two-year stint in the army. I had developed a mental discipline which enabled me to rationalize the need to suffer fools and to tolerate bigots and worse. Having always had a tendency toward cerebration, I learned to fashion intellectual redoubts into which to retreat from confrontation with harsh realities. In other words, I adjusted by "inner emigration," as Sir Isaiah Berlin was later to describe withdrawal from intellectual debate, according to

Fred M. Hechinger. This was a skill which many of my cohorts were unable and/or unwilling to develop, as attested to by the legions of comrades whose manhood directed them to take their chances with courts-martial rather than to submit docilely to transparent affronts to their dignity delivered under the subterfuge of "orders."

Soul-Searching

In recent years I have drawn an analogy between my accommodation to the racist U.S. Army of World War II and John Henrik Clarke's explanation of the reason why the Native American is almost extinct but the African-American remains in America in large numbers. Clarke explained that the Native American attempted to respond in kind, and against impossible odds, to the hostile aggression of the white explorers and provided the pretext for the genocide that was visited upon them. Blacks, on the other hand, Clarke said, jollied the whites, buying time—and multiplied in the meantime. In the play *Purlie Victorious*, Ol' Cap'n Stonewall Jackson Cotchipee gives evidence that he suspects that this is what his son Charlie is doing to him when he asks of Charlie, "You trying to get non-violent with me, boy?"

To some extent this explains how I "got over," as the saying goes in the black community. I put out of mind the affronts and humiliations which I experienced and observed, both on the base and off, and did not permit them to drive me to reactions which could only cause me difficulty. Some of my comrades could not manage this and reacted in kind to brutalization by racist officers and their noncommissioned agents. They suffered the consequences of conviction by courts-martial. Today I wonder if those of my comrades who responded in kind, faced the music and took their punishment now have a clearer conscience about it all than I have. Or, I wonder, do they covet the unblemished military service record, with Good Conduct Medal, with which those of us who responded differently were rewarded?

    I am left with gnawing questions. Why didn't I write a letter to the inspector general and place it in one of those special envelopes which our own officers would not censor (or were not supposed to censor)? Why didn't I blow the whistle on some of the things which I observed? Why didn't I ask where in military regulations did it say that one could humiliate a black warrant officer by having him dig a hole in front of the regimental headquarters? Why didn't I exercise one of these peremptory challenges to test the permissibility of imposing a regimen of bread and water on an enlisted man without court-martial, or indeed question its permissibility if it was permissible *with* court-martial? Why didn't I try to find out if army regulations said anywhere that anyone had the authority to deny me the right to go into town on an even date of the month solely on the basis of the fact that I was black?

    I am unable to pinpoint the rationales which informed my behavior, other than the motivation to survive the perils represented by my superior officers. While the answers to these questions are not the kinds of answers that I was called upon to provide to my comrades in my role as company information and education noncommissioned officer,

I wonder why I didn't try to find the answers for my own benefit.

Suffice it to say that when I returned to civilian life in the spring of 1946, I had developed a *modus vivendi* for coping with injustice and had developed a strong sense of self-worth. I had demonstrated to myself—no one else seemed to have noticed—my ability to exist in relative detachment in an environment in which I had little in common with my fellow enlisted men, and nothing whatsoever in common with our officers. This was the Harry B. Dunbar who rejoined his cohort group at New York University in the fall of 1946 and underwent a social and intellectual experience that without a doubt had much to do with what he became as a person and as a professional.

College Life

As was the case in most colleges and universities in this country in 1946, New York University was bursting at the seams with men and women who had returned from military service. We leavened the incoming classes which normally consisted of June high school graduates. Because of us returning veterans, Washington Square was a headier intellectual environment than it would have been without us. This was as true of the black students, or Negro students as we were known then, as it was of the others. As a matter of fact, I wondered why it was that I had not encountered intelligent, well-educated and motivated black people in the army. Many of them had been there, as I had. However, most of them had not been assigned to labor battalions, as

I had. Some of them had been aviation cadets and then had become commissioned officers in the air force. Others had been assigned to other black units with missions and military occupational specialties which required men who were better educated than was required in labor battalions.

In the 1946 to 1949 era the Washington Square campus of New York University was a strong academic center. Renowned scholars were teaching and doing research there. I was privileged to study with some of these outstanding professors, Professor Germaine Brée, a specialist in twentieth-century French literature, among them. The lectures of Professor Maurice Baudin, one of the finest teachers of French literature anywhere, still reverberate in my mind, forty-five years later. Many of my fellow students in many of the courses I took were native speakers of French and set a steep curve for those of us who spoke French as a second language and who had the temerity to major in French. Professor Henri Olinger, a master teacher of teachers, taught us the art of teaching French. It was in this environment that I made the decision to become a professor of French, and it was in this environment that I learned the craft.

During my early undergraduate years, I did not know of any full-time black faculty members at New York University. Jewell Plummer Cobb, a graduate of Talladega College, was a graduate student in biology and served as a teaching assistant. Ann Campbell, who was from Bradley University in Illinois, was teaching English there in a visiting capacity when I began my graduate work or shortly before. By the time I had completed my undergraduate study in 1949, and had begun to take graduate courses,

Apprenticeship to the Life of the Mind 51

blacks had begun to receive appointments to the NYU faculty. Hale Woodruff came from Atlanta University to be professor of art education. Roscoe Brown came to teach physical education and later to be a key figure in the doctoral (Ph.D.) program in the School of Education. Elliott Skinner joined the faculty in the Department of Anthropology. Dr. James Colston, formerly president of Knoxville College in Tennessee, joined the faculty of education and taught there until his appointment as president of Bronx Community College.

At NYU I joined the Christian Association and participated in its freshman camp. I was also active in the NYU chapter of the National Association for the Advancement of Colored People (NAACP) and recall that we invited the Reverend Adam Clayton Powell as a speaker one evening. I remember, too, at the time having decided that he was the most debonair person I had ever seen close up. I also remember that the NYU chapter of the NAACP was reportedly in jeopardy of being infiltrated by communists and that we maintained close contact with the national office of the NAACP as we sought guidance in this matter.

Friendships and Fraternity

I became friendly with Coolidge McCants, who was a member of the track team. He encouraged me to try out for track, and I remember going to practice one day which turned out to be the day that Reginald Pearman, an outstanding middle distance runner, returned to the NYU track team after having been discharged from the army. I never went back. In 1947, after I had completed a year at NYU, Alpha Phi Alpha Fraternity, Inc., came to my attention. Try as I may, I cannot recall who it was that "rushed" me. In any event, I went to the Harlem YMCA on 135th Street in response to the invitation. I date from that day in 1947 the start of a rite of social passage that was the most important in my life. I pledged Alpha and after a year of hazing and probation I was initiated into the fraternity. I have been an active member ever since. Some of those who were in the same pledge group have become some of the closest friends that I have. I became as close as a blood brother to Coolidge McCants. Even after he moved to Washington, D.C., to practice law we maintained a close association. Our friendship lasted throughout his life. Albert Holland, whom I also met in that pledge group, was as close a friend as I have had in this world. He was my attorney as well, until his death in 1993.

The Commons, as the dining hall in the Washington Square Center of NYU was known, was the location of choice in which the black students congregated in those days. Students from all of the downtown schools of the university would come in to see who was there. I remember seeing James "Skiz" Watson, currently judge of the Court of International Trade in New York, there frequently. At the time he was an undergraduate at NYU. All of the black athletes who were then making headlines—Reggie Pearman, Frank Dixon, Fred Burgess, George Starke, Homer Gillis, Warren Halliburton, Stanley Taylor and others—made that scene with regularity. Black students who were socially prominent also made this scene regularly. It was the place to see and to be seen. It was here that I came to know students such as Dixon, Gillis and Halliburton, who, as it turned out, were already members of Alpha Phi Alpha Fraternity. And it was here that some of them came to know me.

Toward the end of my undergraduate years I developed a dossier in the New York University placement service against the day when I would begin seeking a teaching position. During the summer of 1949, Vernon White, the assistant to the president of Rust College, a black college in Holly Springs, Mississippi, which was run by the Methodist Church, came to New York University to recruit faculty. The placement service referred me to him for consideration for a position as an instructor in French. While I was not yet really ready to take a teaching position out of town, I did meet with Mr. White and succumbed to his strong appeal to my sense of responsibility to contribute to the higher education of blacks. I accepted a position as instructor in French at Rust and went there in September 1949 to begin my career as a college teacher.

CHAPTER 4

Sojourn in the Confederacy

1949–1954

Mississippi

Rust College was a small institution, with a faculty of no more than thirty and a student body of about 300, most of them from rural Mississippi. Located on Highway 78 about seventy miles south of Memphis, the college was one of the most isolated places in which I had ever been. Holly Springs at night is among the darkest spots which I can recall. The two or three students from Chicago, one of whom was an outstanding fullback on the football team, represented the strong influence of the Rust College alumni there. The faculty, not particularly strong in credentials, came largely from Mississippi, Arkansas and Tennessee. There were three of us "outsiders" who were young, and who, in retrospect, seem to me to have been there at that time because the college was about to be reviewed for accreditation by the Southern Association of Schools and Colleges. We probably represented an effort to bring on some people with fairly strong credentials. One, Mamie Morris, was a very bright young woman with a degree in biology from the University of Wisconsin. She came from a distinguished family in Louisville, where her father, a Harvard Ph.D., was a professor of political science at Louisville Municipal College. (This was the college for blacks in Louisville. Blacks could not attend the University of Louisville.) A second was Charles Beasley, a young music teacher from Minneapolis who was a graduate of a music school there. I was the third in this cohort group of young Turks.

Of the senior members of the faculty whom I remember, Professor Rufus Dorsey stands out. He, Beasley, David Wilburn, the registrar, and I shared a cottage on campus. Our main diversion was listening to Professor Dorsey's tales inspired by his odyssey through the Methodist college system for blacks. While he seemed to me at the time to be a very old man, he must have been in his late fifties. A graduate of Clark College in Atlanta with a master's degree from the University of Wisconsin and considerable study beyond, he was the lead man in Rust College's Division of Social Sciences. It seemed to me that he had taught in every black college in the Methodist system, knew everyone who had taught in the system, and had strong opinions about them and the institutions. I was left with the impression that his caustic assessments extended to some of our colleagues at Rust. I reserved and still do reserve judgment on them. Since I stayed at Rust for only one academic year, I was in no position to make a real assessment of them. However, there is one assessment that I feel capable of making about the outcomes of our collective academic effort.

I believe that as a faculty our impact on those students who came to Rust as freshmen in the fall of 1949 was impressive. I remember several of them whom I met in September, who were most remarkable for being "country," the term used to describe the unsophisticated, rural types that they were. Those same students were different young people by the time the middle of the spring quarter rolled around. I attribute the salutary change in the direction of greater sophistication in these students to the effect we had on them in that campus environment. I can attribute it to no other factor, given that isolated environment in which they were quarantined, so to speak. I came away from Rust College with the distinct impression that I had experienced at first hand the difference an institution with only modest resources could make on its students. From that I extrapolated my own mental model of the black college mission statement: "We take them from where they are to where they ought to be." Professor Dorsey seemed to share this feeling. I don't know what intellectual impact, if any, I had personally, on students at Rust. However, I was credited with starting a fad among the young men. I favored bow ties which had to be tied by the wearer and I wore them frequently. I was told that the number of young men who began wearing them on campus on occasions when male students were required to wear ties (at chapel for instance) was the result of my example. Some were known to wear them when ties were not required.

At the end of the 1949–1950 academic year I returned to New York University and enrolled in summer session graduate courses, working toward a master's degree. I met several classmates who became my colleagues in my new career as college teacher of French. They too were teachers of French in black colleges. One of them was a professor at Claflin College in South Carolina; another was at Arkansas Agricultural, Mechanical and Normal (AM&N) College in Pine Bluff. The latter, who was a classmate in an advanced French literature class, told me of an opening for an instructor of French at Dunbar Junior College (DJC) in Little Rock, Arkansas. The position paid more than I had been paid at Rust. Further, it was located in a city of more than 60,000, a far cry from Holly Springs! The dean of this college, who was completing his doctorate in educational administration at New York University, was in residence there for the summer and was interviewing candidates for the position. My classmate brought the two of us together. As a result, I signed on as an instructor of French at Paul Laurence Dunbar Junior College and went there in September 1950 to continue my career.

The fall of 1950 saw the start of careers in black higher education by several members of my peer group at NYU. Rudolph Walker, who majored in industrial arts education, went to Langston University in Oklahoma as an instructor that fall. Warren Halliburton and Thomas Watkins went to Prairie View Agricultural and Mechanical (A&M) College in Prairie View, Texas, to teach English and industrial arts, respectively. Ernest Briggs came to Little Rock, Arkansas, to teach physics at Philander Smith College. Roy Crawford came to Little Rock to teach social sciences at Arkansas

Baptist College. (As a matter of fact, he traveled there with me in my automobile. Since he did not drive, I drove every mile of the way.) Uriel Jackson went to Texas Southern College in Houston to teach history. None of these men made a career of college teaching, however. Walker left Langston for the public schools of St. Louis, where he became a high school teacher and later an administrator. Halliburton became a writer and worked for a publisher as well. Watkins went to work for a Fortune 500 company, first in Westchester County and later in Connecticut. Jackson and Briggs returned to New York State. Jackson became a high school teacher of history in New York City and Briggs a physicist for General Electric in Utica, New York. I lost track of Crawford.

Arkansas

Little Rock was an exciting place in the 1950s. It had a vibrant black community with a sizable and progressive middle class. While the educational system was segregated and the black schools were not funded on a par with those for whites, in my opinion, the black schools were very effective by any measure of outcomes one might use. Dunbar High School, founded in 1929, and, I believe, the only black high school in the state which was fully accredited by the North Central Association of Colleges and Schools, was, in my view, the flagship of the secondary school systems serving blacks in the Southwest. I believe that per capita, this high school produced on a par with the outstanding black high schools of Washington, D.C., and Atlanta, though it does not appear to have received the recognition that it merited. Dr. Faustine Childress Jones, a graduate of Dunbar High School and a member of the education faculty of Howard University, has written an excellent book on the institution.

Opportunity for higher education for blacks in Little Rock was provided by four black colleges. Paul Laurence Dunbar Junior College was an extension of the public school system and had also been founded in 1929. In 1950 it conducted classes in some army surplus buildings across the street from Dunbar High School. Arkansas Baptist College was a small Independent Baptist institution with perhaps 300 students. Shorter College in North Little Rock was a small college operated by the African Methodist Episcopal Church and served perhaps 300 students. Philander Smith College, the crown jewel of Little Rock's higher-education system for blacks, was operated by the United Methodist Church. At the time, it had a very strong and diversified interracial faculty, some of whom had been educated in Europe. There was a significant number of Ph.D.s from strong graduate schools. Philander drew students from a wide area in the Southwest and from across the nation. The intellectual fervor on the campus was phenomenal.

My teaching assignment at Dunbar Junior College involved conducting five sections of an elementary French course. I found the students to be more sophisticated than those I had taught at Rust. My belief is that this was due to the fact that the experiences, both social and educational, that these Dunbar Junior College students had undergone before coming to college were a cut above those that the students at Rust had had. Most of these students had come from Dunbar High School, across the street, or from Jones

High School, the black high school in North Little Rock. Both of these high schools were obviously more challenging educational institutions than those from which most of the students at Rust had come. Life in a large city such as Little Rock also provided a sophistication to these students which rural Mississippi communities did not afford.

I was assigned two extracurricular activities which enabled me to interact with students in informal settings. I was the dramatic coach for the college's entry in the annual dramatic tournament sponsored each year by Sigma Gamma Rho Sorority. In this event, each of the black colleges in the city, as well as AM&N College, the state college for blacks in Pine Bluff, would enter a one-act play in the tournament. A panel of judges would evaluate the performances and award trophies. My troupe won the first-place trophy one year. From that I learned that enthusiastic novices can sometimes outpace experienced performers. I, who had never been a Thespian and who had never before directed a dramatic effort, put together a troupe of two-year college students that defeated other institutions, all of which were four-year institutions, including AM&N, whose coach was a distinguished graduate of the Yale School of Drama. I am the first to recognize that my success was probably more of a tribute to the effectiveness of Mrs. Vivian Hegwood, a drama teacher at Dunbar High School, under whom most of these students had studied as high school students, than to any talent of mine. I think that my troupe's success was but one example of the caliber of the educational program at Dunbar High School.

I was also the debating team coach at Dunbar Junior College. Here again we were always in competition with four-year colleges and here as well we held our own. One year we went on a tour through Texas and debated with college teams there. I do not remember too much about any of the debates. I do remember that one of the most articulate and effective debaters I had on my team was a young woman named Harryette Elam. Until many years later, I did not know what had become of her after she left DJC, though I believed she had gone on to Philander Smith College. One day during President Nixon's administration, I read in *Jet* magazine that Ms. Elam was a highly placed administrative assistant in the White House. In 1992, again in *Jet* magazine, I read that she was the highest-ranking black in the U.S. Information Agency and that she was posted in Afghanistan at the time. Her brother, who had been a high school classmate of my wife, became a psychiatrist and president of Meharry Medical College in Nashville.

When I arrived in Little Rock in 1950 I found Pi Lambda chapter of Alpha Phi Alpha Fraternity, a very active and flourishing graduate chapter. Several of the most prominent and influential black professional men in Little Rock were active members of Pi Lambda. As Eta chapter in New York had been the venue for my readjustment into my social and cultural peer group after my return from military service, Pi Lambda chapter was the venue for my induction into the black professional culture in Little Rock.

Dr. G. W. S. Ish, a distinguished physician, a graduate of Talladega College and Harvard Medical School, John Robert Booker, a veteran attorney and one of the most outgoing personalities I have ever met, Ozell Sutton, the first black reporter for the *Arkansas Democrat,* Jackie L. Shropshire, who I believe was the second black graduate of the

University of Arkansas School of Law, and Dr. M. Lafayette Harris, the president of Philander Smith College were some of the prominent men who were members and who welcomed me warmly into that fellowship. John R. Booker put his personal credit standing behind my application for retail credit accounts in Little Rock. Ozell Sutton was another who was helpful and supportive. Thirty-five years later, I got the opportunity to demonstrate my gratitude to him. When he ran for the national presidency of Alpha Phi Alpha Fraternity, I led his campaign effort in New York. When he was elected, he appointed me as co-chair of the fraternity's election commission. I remained active on this commission after my term as chair and indeed have participated in some way in the activities of this commission ever since. One of my colleagues at Dunbar Junior College, William Gilkey, a young man of my age, who had grown up in Little Rock and had attended Tennessee State College, where he had been initiated into Alpha Phi Alpha Fraternity, came back to teach science at Dunbar Junior College and joined the faculty along with me in September 1950. He also joined Pi Lambda chapter with me that same year. We became inseparable friends. I was best man at his wedding in Little Rock. He left teaching and ultimately became employee benefit manager for the Thrifty Drug Store chain in California. We still remain in contact. When he comes east and when I go to California we see each other. We had a particularly nostalgic reunion in Los Angeles in 1992 when I experienced a fulfilling period of retrospection with him and Thomas B. Shropshire, another Alpha, native of Little Rock and retired senior vice-president of Miller Beer.

The annual black-tie ball which Pi Lambda chapter held each year after Christmas was one of the top social affairs in Little Rock. Students from colleges across the country who were home on Christmas vacation would be there. All the socially prominent black people in Little Rock and from elsewhere would be there. I was there.

However, life in Little Rock was not without its encounters with the reality of racial prejudice. One day I went to the U.S. Employment Service in downtown Little Rock to answer an advertisement which had appeared in either the *Gazette* or the *Democrat,* the Little Rock dailies. This ad was recruiting persons with college degrees in foreign languages to work in Washington, D.C. Since I had a bachelor's and a master's degree in French and was teaching French on the college level, I arrogated to myself qualification to pursue this employment possibility. When I walked into the office and told the receptionist why I was there she did not know quite how to deal with me. She excused herself and went into a back office. She returned with a man who was obviously her supervisor. He asked me what it was that had brought me there. I told him that I had seen the newspaper advertisement seeking applicants for some entry-level positions in foreign languages. His response to me, though I did not know it at the time, would later make me a staunch advocate of affirmative action. He told me that they were indeed seeking such applicants, but said, "We don't have anything to go on for colored." It was with great satisfaction that I received a clipping from the *Arkansas Gazette* of March 2, 1962, sent to me by my brother-in-law, announcing: "Two Negroes went to work for the Arkansas Employment Security Division, yesterday, the first 'white collar' workers of their race to be employed by the ESD."

Ernest Briggs, my former NYU college mate and Alpha Phi Alpha Fraternity brother, and his wife lived in a small cottage near the Philander Smith campus. They often invited me to dinner and I spent a good deal of time with them in their home. Through them I met Maurice Mynatt, a young professor of education at Philander Smith. He was a single man and lived in one of the men's dormitories where he was nominally in charge. I often would go there to meet him when we were going out together with others.

I came to know one of the students in that dormitory in a most unusual way. I don't remember his name, but I do remember that he was called "T-Town," because he hailed from Tulsa.

T-Town had a habit of standing in the corridor of the dormitory, leaning over a rail and speaking to no one in particular for minutes at a time. I observed him doing this on more than one occasion. When I noticed him the first time, I thought that he was practicing a presentation which he was to make for a speech course. It became obvious to me on subsequent visits that this was not the case. One day after I knew that T-Town realized that I was a friend of Professor Mynatt and when I felt that he would not be offended by my question, I asked him what he was doing. He responded that he was soliloquizing. He said that when you soliloquized you were not speaking to anyone, but anyone could listen. Moreover, he posited that you could talk about anything that you were thinking about. It did not have to fit into any particular context. T-Town, leaning over a railing in the veterans' dormitory of Philander Smith

College more than forty years ago, provided a rationale for me for this rambling memoir.

At the Briggs' home I became friendly with another member of the Philander Smith College faculty. He was Charles D. Henry, a professor of physical education, who, over time, turned out to have one of the sharpest minds among my associates. As our friendship grew, he convinced me that it was not appropriate that the two of us were roomers in the homes of others, fine homes though they were. What we needed, Henry argued, was an apartment. He went on to give a rationale to which I had not given even passing consideration before. He and I were eligible bachelors, he said. One of the prime requisites which defined an eligible bachelor, Henry informed me, was a place to entertain his friends. So it was that Charles D. Henry and Harry B. Dunbar took a beautiful apartment together in an upscale neighborhood in Little Rock. Henry and I maintained this accoutrement of our status until Winthrop Rockefeller came to Little Rock, bringing with him a black aide who required digs which befitted his status. Our apartment fitted the bill just right and we were forced to relinquish it.

Forebodings

Several years later, when the U.S. Supreme Court was considering the question of separate but equal education, I was still teaching at Dunbar Junior College. The thought occurred to me that when the Court decided the case, if it found against the doctrine of separate but equal, one result would be a single junior college in Little Rock and I would be competing with my white counterparts for a teaching position. I wondered if those who would be making the staffing decisions in the merger would "have anything to go on for colored." I did not stay around to find out, but returned to New York to pursue a doctoral degree in my field. It was of interest to me to note later that Little Rock reportedly resolved its dilemma by selling Little Rock Junior College to a foundation for $1 and closing Dunbar Junior College.

An article in the *Arkansas Gazette* of April 8, 1955, reported the closing of Dunbar Junior College. The article confirmed my suspicions of late 1953 and permitted me to conclude that I had been wise in taking my leave of the institution in January of 1954. (The school board of the City of Little Rock sat as the Board of Trustees of Dunbar Junior College. This board also sat as the Board of Trustees for Little Rock Junior College, the institution that was maintained for white students. At the time, all members of the school board of the City of Little Rock were white.) The *Gazette* reported that a secret meeting of the Board of Trustees of Dunbar Junior College was held on March 28, at which meeting a resolution was adopted to abolish the institution effective May 27. No announcement of the decision was made until April 7 and no explanation was given for the delay.

The news story stated that the lack of adequate finances and the competition from other institutions made the continuance of the school impossible. Dr. E. Baron, the president of the Board of Trustees of Dunbar Junior College, said that Dunbar was intended to be entirely self-supporting. Since tuition and fees weren't sufficient to meet operating costs, the college must be closed as it would be unlawful to use public funds to make up the difference. Dr. Baron saw no alternative to closing the institution.

An alternative which I would have found not only feasible but eminently desirable would have been to integrate the Little Rock Junior College (LRJC) by folding in the meager resources which Dunbar had and transferring the 304 students there. However, in his comments to the reporter Dr. Baron is quoted as saying, "LRJC is a private college and there hasn't been any thought of admitting Negroes there." Neither was there any intention to integrate Donaghey College, the proposed successor to Little Rock Junior College, the *Gazette* article informed us.

My question is whether Dunbar Junior College was not also a private college and in exactly the same legal circumstance as Little Rock Junior College. Further, my question is—When did LRJC become a private college? It would be interesting to trace the legal maneuvering that went on to take the Little Rock Junior College out of the orbit of integration while Dunbar Junior College was being quietly abolished. Every time I go to Little Rock and drive by the magnificent buildings and grounds of the University of Arkansas at Little Rock, the presumptive descendant of Little Rock Junior College, I fantasize about what might have been in my own career. I guess the Board of Trustees "didn't have anything to go on for colored."

CHAPTER 5

Full Man, Ready Man, Exact Man

The 1954–1964 decade was the one in which I was married, moved back to New York City, became a father, solidified my education, mastered the art of teaching, became fully credentialed for the professoriate and came to the threshold of a rewarding career as a college teacher and administrator. Most significantly, my personal, social and philosophical orientation as a black man was synthesized and coordinated with my intellectual formation. Prior to leaving Little Rock in late January of 1954 I married Cora Charlene Whitlow, who is from an old Little Rock family and a graduate of Philander Smith College. She was working as a secretary in a Little Rock office of the Arkansas Agricultural Extension Service when I met her.

Charlene had spent her entire life in Little Rock, had attended public schools there and graduated from Dunbar High School and from Dunbar Junior College, before attending Philander Smith and graduating in 1950 with a major in business. I am often reminded by events of how her life and circle of friends reflects a kind of stability in a single community and shared childhoods that is the antithesis of my own. She lived all of her life at the same address in the west end of Little Rock, in a home owned by her parents. Nearly all of her close friends go back to her neighborhood and her elementary school days. While most of them have left Little Rock for Los Angeles, Detroit, Bakersfield, and Chicago, they are still close; she sees them and has visits from them when we are in those cities and when they and she are back in Little Rock to visit. When they get together, or even when they talk on the telephone, there is a celebration of common experience which I do not know from personal experience.

With stops in St. Louis and Indianapolis, the drive from Little Rock to Baisley Park in Queens, where we planned to live temporarily with my sister Louise and her husband Al, served as our honeymoon. New York was in the midst of a mini-recession in early 1954 and the only work I could find was as a porter in the Gertz department store in Jamaica, Queens. I worked there until late in the spring when I landed a provisional position as a playground director for the Department of Parks of the City of New York in the Bayside section of Queens. In the fall I began work as a substitute teacher in junior high schools in Queens and Manhattan. Shortly thereafter, the Board of Examiners of the Board of Education of the City of New York announced an examination for licensure as permanently appointed teacher of French in the junior high schools. This was the first examination to be given in this discipline since the end of World War II.

The licensure process in the New York City school system was rather rigid at the time. It called for written examinations, one covering education and another covering the particular discipline in which one sought to teach. A speech test was also part of the screening process. A foreign accent, a southern accent, or any linguistic pattern that was not standard American English was cause for elimination. If one survived those tests, a performance test was given in which the applicant taught a class on a topic assigned on the spot by the examiner. As a survivor of the written and speech tests, I was notified to report to a junior high school in Manhattan where an examiner, a matronly, seasoned teacher of French, gave me a topic and an hour or so to prepare a lesson. She sat in the back of the room and observed me as I taught the lesson. Several months later I received notice that I had passed! Now I could expect a permanent assignment as a teacher of French in a junior high school somewhere in New York City.

As was the custom, a list of persons who had passed this examination and examinations in other disciplines was published on the education page of the *New York World Telegram and Sun*. In due course I received an appointment as a charter member of the faculty of Francis Scott Key Junior High School 117, which opened in the Williamsburg section of Brooklyn in the fall of 1955. The appointment was noted on the education page of the *World Telegram and Sun*. I now had a stable position with sufficient income to support my family and to fund my graduate work toward a doctoral degree at New York University. More than that, this position, which required that I teach elementary French to hundreds of students daily, five days a week, enabled me to hone my presentation skills to the point at which I became a master teacher. My performance ratings testified to this. I was tenured in the position in 1958. Moreover, I began to get some of the scarce, much-sought-after assignments to teach in summer sessions in the high schools of the city.

I began the application process for admission to the doctoral program in the Department of Foreign Languages and Literatures of the School of Education at New York University. I took and passed the general qualifying examination, was admitted to matriculated status and began taking courses at night and on Saturdays. Study in this program in the 1950s was an exhilarating experience. I had as teachers some outstanding scholars in French. The program permitted me to take courses in the Graduate School of Arts and Sciences, where I studied under Professors Germaine Brée, Maurice Baudin, and others. In the School of Education I studied under Professors Henri Olinger and Anna Balakian and under Mlle. Cybèle Pomerance, an adjunct instructor who regularly taught in the high schools of New York. She was particularly effective in teaching how to teach French and how to organize course content. Another adjunct instructor who had great influence on me and my development as a teacher and scholar was M. Robert Lacour-Gayet, an eminent French writer and teacher who was, I believe, a permanent teacher at the Collège de France in Paris. His *La France au Vingtième Siècle*

(*France in the Twentieth Century*), which received high critical acclaim, was published while I was a student of his. His and Professor Germaine Brée's recommendations were significant helps to me in France when I went there to research my dissertation. My apprenticeship to these scholars was the proximate impetus to my success as a college teacher. I was able to customize a program of study to further my personal interests in the art of teaching and in French literature and civilization.

Research Focus

During my coursework in French, I became aware of the incidence of great French writers and university professors who had been trained at the Ecole normale supérieure ("Higher Normal School") on the *rue d'Ulm* ("Ulm Street") in Paris. I discovered that this institution was undoubtedly one of the greatest intellectual forcing beds in Europe. My interest in teaching as an art, in outstanding educational institutions, and my wide readings in French literature and history made me a ready man on the subject of *l'esprit normalien* (the temperament of students of the Ecole normale supérieure), the scholarly mark with which the Ecole normale reputedly branded its students. I informed one of my instructors, M. Robert Lacour-Gayet, who had a close relative who was a graduate of the Ecole normale, of my interest in doing a study on this institution as my doctoral project. M. Lacour-Gayet suggested that I talk with Professor Jean Albert Bédé of Columbia University, who was himself a graduate of the institution; M. Lacour-Gayet provided me with an introduction to Professor Bédé. I went to Columbia University and met with Professor Bédé. The result of our discussion was that Professor Bédé agreed that it was a feasible dissertation topic and I received approval for a dissertation on the topic "The Impact of the *Ecole normale supérieure* on Selected Men of Letters of France, 1875–1902." I was sponsored by a committee of distinguished scholars, consisting of Professor William Brickman, an eminent educational historian who was the chair, Professor Germaine Brée, a renowned scholar in twentieth-century French literature, and Dr. James Hanscom, a specialist in diplomatic history. This group of eminent scholars guided me through the most meaningful intellectual experience of my life.

Enigmas

In most of the courses in French that I took, I had challenging intellectual experiences dealing with the ideas of men of letters such as Descartes and Rousseau, Proust and Péguy, Talleyrand and de Gaulle, to name but a few. In reflecting on the ideas and concepts that I engaged and that engaged me as a graduate student and even as a teacher of lower-division French courses, two residual themes remain with me for continuing study. Interestingly, they are not weighty ones that one recalls from, say, Descartes but rather simple ones from two works. The first was inspired by *L'Etranger* (*The Stranger*), a work of that student of the absurd, Albert Camus. I have, since I read it forty years ago, been intrigued by the theme of estrangement that permeates this work. I was, and am, obsessed with the notion of drawing every ounce of substance from *L'Etranger* and in particular from the estrangement of the protagonist Meursault. I have reread this volume many times and have taught it, once in a high school advanced-placement course and several times in elementary courses in colleges.

The second residual theme that has endured with me since my graduate school days is the search for meanings in one of the works of an airline pilot who wrote when time and circumstances permitted. I have a twin obsession to plumb the possible depths of meaning to be found in several passages in Antoine de Saint-Exupéry's *Le Petit Prince* (*The Little Prince*). I am reassured by an aphorism, attributed to Saint-Exupéry, to the effect that "the meaning of things lies not in the things themselves but in our attitude towards them."* Perhaps I have already found the ultimate meaning or meanings to be found in the work of Antoine de Saint-Exupéry. But I intend to explore further when time permits.

My appetite for extracting meaning from texts was whetted while I was a graduate student at NYU. The skills, techniques and stimulus to engage in this didactic exercise were learned from the example of M. Robert Lacour-Gayet, one of my teachers in the Department of Foreign Languages and Literatures of the School of Education at NYU. This method of teaching literary works, known as *l'explication de texte* ("textual analysis"), a standard teaching tool in the university system of France, and in better departments of French in American universities as well, was

---

*From "Bridge," *Rockland Journal-News*, Jan. 18, 1993, p. C2.

employed with great skill by M. Lacour-Gayet. It requires the teacher to have a thorough knowledge of the life, thought, writings and times of the author of the work being taught. I recall reading, many years ago, a tribute being paid to Morris Raphael Cohen by a student who was rhapsodizing about the resounding and brilliant explications delivered by Cohen at the City College of New York, explications which made literary works come to life for him. I am one of the many students at New York University for whom M. Robert Lacour-Gayet did the same.

Studying Abroad

In 1956 I applied for and was granted a special Fulbright Award to participate in a six-week summer seminar for American high school teachers of French and junior members of college faculties. It was conducted at the Sorbonne in Paris. Thirty of us, four of whom were black, constituted the group selected. Of the four blacks, three of us were graduate students at New York University and knew each other there. Miss Era Brisbane was teaching in one of the junior high schools in Manhattan and I was teaching at Francis Scott Key Junior High School in Brooklyn. We were pursuing the doctorate in the same department at NYU and had taken some courses together, at least one with M. Lacour-Gayet. The third black member of the group was Virgil Wright, a teacher of French at Jarvis Christian College in Texas. He also was a graduate student in French in the department along with Era Brisbane and me. The fourth black member of the contingent was Paul

McGirt, a member of the French faculty at North Carolina College in Durham and a student in the doctoral program in French at Western Reserve University in Ohio.

The program which was conceived for us at *l'Ecole de préparation et de perfectionnement des professeurs de français à l'étranger* ("School for the Training and Improvement of Teachers of French from Abroad"), an institute of the Sorbonne, was an excellent one. We had classroom lectures by professors at the institute. We took excursions to historical sites in Paris and to the chateau country in the Loire Valley, where we listened to lectures by professors from the Sorbonne who accompanied us on the excursions. One of the instructors that I had there was the nephew of Gustave Lanson, one of the men of letters whom I included in my dissertation.

The examinations which we underwent at the end of the seminar were administered in classically French university style. They were partly written and partly oral. The orals were administered by a jury of professors who had not taught us. We were ranked from 1 to 10 on most subjects, with 1 being the lowest and 10 being the highest rating. A large certificate, bearing the raised seal of the Sorbonne, was awarded at the end, with one's ratings in each subject listed and one's ranking in the group recorded thereon. My certificate did much for my ego as well, testifying as it does that I ranked fifth among the thirty participants in the seminar and that it was awarded to me with *Mention Très Honorable* (with honors). I rate my experience as a participant in the Fulbright program as a significant part of my credentialing as a college teacher of French.

I returned to New York in August. During that very

month, the defiance of the court-ordered desegregation of Central High School in Little Rock began to unfold. It was with a sense of personal involvement that Charlene and I followed this eerie story on television and in the newspapers. She saw the sons and daughters of her friends and former neighbors in Little Rock as they underwent aggression by white citizens. I felt involved as well, having met, known and admired Mrs. Daisy Bates, the mentor to the black children involved. Charlene and I derive some satisfaction from the fact that some of those nine young people have achieved personal and professional success despite the ugly, psyche-scarring experience. Our hearts go out to those whose untold stories suggest that others of the nine did not fare well.

 In the fall of 1957, I returned to my teaching duties at Junior High 117 and my graduate work at New York University. I developed a research design for my dissertation and it was approved by my sponsoring committee. My hypothesis was that the *Ecole normale* on the *rue d'Ulm* in Paris, a rigid academic environment presided over by a cadre of brilliant scholars, which admitted, by means of a rigorous academic competition, thirty or so very able young men per year, "the cream of the cream" of the current high school graduates of any given year, put an intellectual mark on these young men that set them apart from the rest of their cohort group in France and made them eminently distinguishable from all others. This mark, commonly referred to as *l'esprit normalien,* was, I hypothesized, a Gallic Ivy League mind-set. My research design was calculated to demonstrate this phenomenon as it operated on generations of young intellects during the Third Republic from

1875–1902, as exemplified in the cases of seven selected former students: Baudrillart, Bédier, Bergson, Jaurès, Lanson, Péguy, and Rolland.

One of the courses that I took was a tool course in historiography under Dr. William Brickman, who was an eminent educational historian and the chair of my sponsoring committee. This course was a linchpin in my development as a researcher. Prior to the time that I took it, my training had been exclusively in language and literature. The dissertation by its very nature required that I use historical techniques to develop the backdrop which constituted the intellectual forces and influences which were the *Ecole normale* and, I contended, marked the seven literary figures. It was in discussions with Dr. Brickman that I was persuaded that tracking intellectual influence was a difficult, if not impossible, task to accomplish within the bounds of historical standards. The likelihood of finding satisfactory documentation to justify a claim of having established influence, Dr. Brickman argued, was not great for even one of the seven selected former students, much less for all seven. This explains my use of the more modest word "impact" rather than the word "influence" in the ultimate title of my study. It also fixes in my mind a citation in Dr. Brickman's manual on educational history to the effect that when the sources are silent the wise do not speak. I still have this manual on the bookshelf in my home office and consult it regularly when I am working on scholarly pieces. I feel compelled to say here that any care that I exercise in making claims in this book about events that I did not witness is in large part a result of the teaching and example of Professor William Brickman and that any breaches of the canons of historical research that I commit represent instances when I should have consulted his work again, but did not.

I conducted the research for my investigation in two of the great research libraries of the western world: the New York Public Library in Manhattan and the *Bibliothèque nationale* ("National Library") in Paris. Moreover, I was privileged to have access to the archives of the *Ecole normale* and was extended courtesies there that probably are normally enjoyed only by senior scholars. I attribute this to a letter of introduction to the librarian of the *Ecole normale* provided to me by Professor Germaine Brée, a distinguished world-class literary figure in her own right, who was a member of my sponsoring committee. Doing research in these three environments and rubbing elbows with other serious scholars was a significant experience for me.

Some time in 1958, I applied for and was awarded a John Hay Whitney Opportunity Fellowship from the John Hay Whitney Foundation to support an academic year of research in France. These were fellowships which the foundation awarded annually to black academics and to others to provide the opportunity for awardees to achieve in areas where they had demonstrated promise. The award was for the academic year 1959-1960 and permitted me to go to France and consult the rich sources available there on the *Ecole normale* and its graduates. By that time I had become a tenured teacher in the New York City Public School System. I took my modest savings, the John Hay Whitney Opportunity Fellowship, my wife and my five-year-old daughter, and sailed from New York on September 9, 1959, aboard the SS *Atlantic* for Zeebrugge, Belgium, and a year's unpaid leave devoted to research in France.

CHAPTER 6

Sojourn in the Fifth Republic

Life on Foreign Soil

When the ship docked in Zeebrugge, we took the opportunity to go to Brussels for a few days to visit with Gwendolyn McCants Mabry, her husband Ralph and their children, who were there because Ralph was in medical school at the University of Brussels. I knew Ralph only slightly, but I knew Gwen well, since her brother Coolidge and I were very good friends. We had been college mates at New York University and had been initiated into Alpha Phi Alpha Fraternity together in 1948. From our visit with them I came to have a very high regard for Ralph's intelligence, focus and determination. I left Brussels for Paris with a considerably reduced sense of self-satisfaction at the sacrifice and risk that I was taking by going to France with a wife and child with only a fellowship and meager savings to tide us over. After all, I knew the language which was the medium for the study that I was undertaking. Further, I knew that my sojourn would be for but one academic year. Ralph, on the other hand, had grown up in Harlem, spoke only English, and had attended City College there in Harlem. For him to go to medical school in Brussels, where instruction was in French and Flemish, and to do so with very little money, three young children, and no Flemish at all represented a tremendous leap of faith on his part. He knew that his rite of passage was to take at least six years and that his entire professional future was at risk if he failed. In my case there was the secure tenure-protected position as a teacher of French that I would return to in the New York City Public Schools.

We did not see Ralph and Gwen again until in the 1970s when their daughter was married in New York, but it was not until 1992 that we had the occasion to have a real visit with them. Over the Thanksgiving weekend that year we were in Las Vegas where they live and where Ralph now practices medicine. Their children were grown. We went to their home and spent a nostalgic afternoon and evening with them. I came away that night with the feeling that their unique Belgian experience of the early 1960s had bonded them in a special way and had made of Ralph a very special type of physician, had made of Gwen a very special type of wife and mother and had made their children a unique group of young adults.

We went on to Paris and to the little northern suburban community called Bécon-les-Bruyères, where we had an excellent and comfortable apartment on the second floor in a well-kept building. Bécon-les-Bruyères adjoins another community called Courbevoie, where we enrolled our soon-to-be-five-year-old daughter in the *école maternelle* (kindergarten) a short walk from our apartment. My daily commute into Paris was a civilized experience. The railroad line that connected the Bécon-les-Bruyères and Courbevoie communities with the *Gare St. Lazare* ("St. Lazare Station") in Paris was reliable. The trains ran regularly and on time. As I recall, the commute took about half an hour. Another ten or fifteen minutes on the Metro put me at the *Bibliothèque nationale* within an hour of having left home.

Working in the cavernous high-ceilinged reading room next to persons who certainly included renowned scholars, putting books in bundles to be set aside for my use on the next day when I would return, riffling through the ancient handwritten file cards in the card catalog drawers and filling out requests in one of the greatest research libraries in the world, calling for books dating back hundreds of years, was a heady experience for me.

While researching my dissertation in the *Bibliothèque nationale* I came across a series of pseudonymous essays signed "Fidus" which appeared in the *Revue des deux mondes*. At the time I believed that the series consisted of the twelve "*Silhouettes Contemporaines,*" which I discovered in the *Bibliothèque nationale* in 1960 and which had been published in the review between January 15, 1920, and February 1, 1928. I made a resolve to pursue the question of who Fidus really was and wrote an article offering some hypotheses on the subject. My article was published in the *French Review* in 1961. It elicited a letter from Professor Edward Harvey of Kenyon College who himself had been intrigued by the subject at one time. He sent me boilerplate proof that he had established that one of these essays had been written by André Bellessort. I have continued to be interested in this matter, have pursued it when time permitted and have determined that the complete series of the Fidus papers consists of more than thirty essays. I have collected photocopies of thirty-four of them. Other articles I wrote on the subject were published in the spring 1966 and fall 1967 issues of *Concord,* the faculty magazine at New York City Community College. In the spring of 1966 I received a research grant from the State University of New York to support my research of this subject. I gave a lecture on the subject at Bergen Community College in 1985. My hypothesis is that at least three hands authored these essays. One day I expect to have more to say on this subject.

Creature of habit that I am, I began going daily to eat lunch in a modest restaurant near the *Biblothèque nationale.* The same people frequented it every day. I came to know two men who lunched there regularly. One, M. Louis Durand, a man of perhaps the same age as I, thirty-four, was a stagehand at the *Comédie Française.* The other, surnamed Bailly, whose first name I cannot recall, was a mature man, probably in his fifties, an attorney. (Durand and I both referred to him as "*maître* Bailly.") I felt that I had really arrived when I came to be considered a regular at their table and my napkin was put in a ring after meals and put away with theirs to be put on "our" table the next day. The three of us discussed all manner of subjects during those lunch hours. They would question me about matters in the United States. I would question them about matters current in France. I am still a little amused at the way these men used to talk about how we Americans approached certain issues and how they included me among "*vous autres*

Anglos-Saxons" ("you Anglo-Saxons"). It was a rather sad leave-taking when I told them that I would not be joining them for lunch any more because my schedule called for me to go to the *Ecole normale* and do some work in its archives.

The librarian at the *Ecole normale* welcomed me, took me down to the archives in the basement, showed me around and gave me the "run of the house." He also gave me a set of the annual yearbooks of the association of former students, which is nearly a complete run dating from 1902 to 1953. Handwritten documents from which history is written abounded in those archives. Most of these were not catalogued in any way, so one had to go through a great deal of paper to find things that were relevant. This was in itself a good experience for me. The result of this was that, using historical research methods, I wrote and successfully defended a dissertation of 409 pages. It was not without considerable disappointment that I read in the *New York Times* of April 5, 1971, not only that M. Robert Flacelière, the director of the *Ecole normale supérieure,* had resigned during a takeover by students of the New Left but that a fire in the basement had destroyed some archives of the institution. I felt as disappointed as I would have had I heard that the incident had happened at New York University. Some of the documents which I cite in my dissertation, I thought, are probably gone forever.

I believe that spending the academic year 1959–1960 in France was a good experience for my family, as it was for me. Our daughter became fluent in French and adjusted to life in a French *école maternelle*. She was the only black child there, though not the only one whose first language was English. One of her classmates was from Ireland and spoke

English. However, by Christmas one would never have known that either of the two was not a native speaker of French. As a matter of fact my daughter Nona was embarrassed by my wife's use of English in the company of other parents and requested that she speak French. The one major adjustment that Nona had to make was to the discovery, made in a French butcher shop, that chicken does not originate in styrofoam boxes covered with clear plastic wrap. She had not made this discovery in four and one-half years of life in Brooklyn. Had she not gone to live in Bécon-les-Bruyères, who knows when she would have found this out. Charlene, for her part, good soldier that she was and is, adjusted well to the difficulties of living in a culture that was totally different from the one in which she had grown up. Before long she shopped in the groceries, bakeries, butcher shops and the like with skill, if not with ease.

The only time we frequented the American community while we were in France was on Sundays when we made our weekly pilgrimage to the American Church in Paris. James and Joyce Potgieter, a young American couple from Iowa whom we had met on the ship and who were on a tour of Europe, visited us in Bécon-les-Bruyères. He was a grain dealer from Steamboat Rock, Iowa. She was an elementary school teacher. They were very friendly people. My recollection is that he had done a year of study at the London School of Economics after graduating from Reed College, a highly selective liberal arts college. We exchanged Christmas cards with the Potgieters for many years afterward. They included a newsletter about themselves each year.

Richard Wright, the author, is the only black American I recall seeing during our sojourn in France. Charlene reminded me that I had pointed him out to her in services at the American Church one Sunday. Most of the blacks I saw were male francophone Africans who were students at the Sorbonne, some of whom were married to white French women. In any case, black family groups of any stripe were not anywhere to be found in the circle in which we moved. The most telling documentation of this is to be found in an experience we had. One day the three of us were in a park. I don't recall whether it was the little park in Bécon-les-Bruyères or in the *Bois de Boulogne*. I saw a child who was probably about Nona's age run up to her mother and say, "*Maman, voilà toute une famille noire*" ("Ma, there is a whole black family"). That youngster probably had seen families in which there was one black member, but ours was the first she had seen where all of the members were black.

Early in June of 1960 we packed our belongings and my precious research notes, and on June 15, 1960, boarded the SS *United States* in Le Havre and sailed for the United States.

Looking back on my experiences as a black in France, I must observe here that I never encountered any unkind or racist behavior or language during any of my time in France, neither in 1944–1945, when I was there as a soldier, nor in 1957 or in 1959–1960, when I moved about in the Paris community and its environs as a civilian.

CHAPTER 7

Engagement to the Cause

Speaking Out

During the summer of 1960 I followed the help-wanted advertisements in the education section of the *New York Times* as I had done habitually, even when not looking for work. I saw an ad recruiting a teacher of French to take over the foreign-language department at the Nanuet Junior-Senior High School in Nanuet, in Rockland County, New York. I was familiar with the county, having lived there from my junior year in high school until I went off to the army. I knew that the school districts in the county were very good and enjoyed good support from the taxpayers. I also knew that the teaching environment was excellent in the Nanuet district. I applied for the position and was selected. I began teaching there in the fall of 1960. We moved from Brooklyn to Spring Valley, New York, where we found an apartment in the section that is now called

"The Hill." Then predominantly Jewish, this area is now a black neighborhood with all of the problems that go with neighborhoods that decline and become totally black.

As I began my new teaching assignment, I continued to synthesize the information I had collected in France and to write my dissertation. While I had been in France I had sent drafts of some of the early chapters to Dr. Brickman in New York. He had made comments and suggestions, which I followed. I now had conferences from time to time with each of the three committee members and I polished the draft in consonance with their advice. During the fall of 1960 I received the approval of all of the members of my sponsoring committee, successfully defended in the spring and was awarded my degree in June of 1961.

My experience at Nanuet High School was a satisfying one. The Department of Foreign Languages consisted of six members and offered French, Latin and Spanish. The district was small, had a good tax base, and was populated by a large number of college-educated people, notably science-oriented persons associated with the Lederle Laboratories, which was located in the district. The students whom I taught were achievers who sought and gained admission to competitive colleges. Teaching them was rewarding. I, the lone black teacher in the high school, was fully accepted. In-school student groups such as the Junior Honor Society invited me to be their speaker, as did the senior Honor Society. Out-of-school groups of the same students, such as the Youth Group of the Nanuet Jewish Center, invited me to speak to them. There was a joke around that I had been to so many bar mitzvahs that I could, unassisted, find my place in the prayer book. I attribute to a speech which I gave at the Nanuet Jewish Center on March 21, 1966, subsequent invitations which I received to speak before other Jewish groups in Rockland County. My topic was "On Being a Negro in America circa 1966: A Personal, Middle-Class View." In this speech I made unapologetic advocacy for integration, for middle-class values, and for an open society where all comers would be treated with justice and equity. I was not timid about placing a share of blame on black parents for the problem of the high incidence of dropouts among black students, as I did in April of 1964 as a participant on an all-black panel consisting of educators and a social worker in Spring Valley.

In reviewing my notes, texts of my speeches, and program notes that I have saved over the years and used in the preparation of these memoirs, I have been impressed with the number of comments which I made in the 1960s and 1970s that are on target even today. I am very disappointed that I cannot find the text of a talk that I gave to a Unitarian Church congregation in my community here in West Nyack. My disappointment is predicated on the fact that I cannot recall a single thing that I said on that Sunday, April 12, 1970, when I spoke on the subject "Black Personality Disorders: The Legacy of White Racism." I suspect that the program chairperson asked me for a copy of it and that I gave it to him or her. Since I did not use a computer to prepare my presentations in the 1970s, and probably prepared only a single typescript, which I used to deliver the speech, whatever I said has in all probability been lost forever.

My colleagues, the Rockland County Foreign Language Teachers Association, also extended their professional recognition to me by electing me as their chairman. Also, while at Nanuet High School I served as a member of a visiting team of the Middle States Association of Schools and Colleges, which evaluated the St. Francis Preparatory School in Brooklyn when it applied for accreditation.

Advocacy

During this period I became very active in the Nyack branch of the National Association for the Advancement of Colored People and became chairman of its education committee. As a consequence of this I became an ombudsman for black parents who were having difficulties with the Nyack School District. The local newspaper covered the meetings and activities of the Nyack NAACP branch very thoroughly. When I spoke on the subject of education or on problems in the black community I was often quoted in the local press. I became a veritable unpaid consultant to the Nyack School District and gave advice to the superintendent of schools and to other administrators on various issues, particularly as they affected black students. I accompanied the assistant superintendent on a recruitment tour in search of black teachers.

We visited Appalachian State College at Boone, North Carolina, and Tennessee Agricultural and Industrial (A&I) State College in Nashville, among others, and talked to prospective candidates. While I would not argue *post hoc, ergo propter hoc,* I believe that the Nyack branch of the NAACP helped improve the diversity of the teaching staff of the Nyack School District. I also had occasion to serve as an ombudsman for a black parent who was also a neighbor and who had engaged in a confrontation with the school district in which I lived, and still live. My daughter Nona was a student in the district at the time. The issue was that of the portrayal of a domestic in a performance at the high school. My neighbor had attended the performance and had been offended by the portrayal of "Mammy Pleasant," a black maid complete with slurred speech, bandana, and all of the stereotypical characteristics of Aunt Jemima. She had gone to school officials and had registered her complaint. She was not satisfied with their dismissal of what they considered to be her unwarranted, misplaced sensitivity in this matter and their ruling that they would pursue the matter no further. My neighbor went to the Nyack NAACP and lodged a complaint. I was dispatched to confer with the superintendent of the Clarkstown schools on this matter.

As I reflect on it now, there were several issues involved. First, there was the issue of the academic freedom of the faculty and students and their right to select a dramatic work from the canon of American dramatic literature and to re-create it as an educational experience for high school students. Second, there was the issue of whether or not a taxpayer who was offended by an activity presented by the high school attended by her daughter had any grounds for having this academic freedom curbed. The superintendent went to great lengths in his effort to persuade me that this woman had no grounds to be offended by the portrayal. I could not get him to understand that neither he nor I had any way of evaluating the genuineness of her sense of offense. I tried to show him that, whatever his or my view was on the situation, the fact was that this woman said she was offended. There was no way that either of us could counter that. He was unmoved by my arguments. When I reported back to the Nyack NAACP branch meeting, the press picked it up and a story was generated about my confrontation with the school district. The fat was in the fire. The result was the inference that I had characterized the school district and/or the superintendent as racist. I received the only poison-pen letter I ever received in the ten or so years that I engaged in civil rights advocacy in the 1960s and 1970s. It was an anonymous letter, postmarked in a northern New Jersey community just over the state line from Rockland County. Written in a feminine hand, it extolled the virtues of the superintendent of schools, upbraided me for my reported excoriation of him, and, in a non sequitur which puzzles me to this day, asked why I live in the neighborhood where I do. My guess is that the questioner wanted to know why I didn't live in a community where blacks were in the majority and where the school district would have to be concerned about how my people were portrayed. Presumably, in her opinion, the Clarkstown School District should not have to concern itself with such matters.

I began to be called upon by civic, religious and other groups to speak and to participate in panel discussions which dealt with important social issues that affected the Rockland County community. I spoke before church groups of various denominations in Rockland and Westchester counties. I spoke before a local group of the American Jewish Congress. In most instances I dealt with some aspect of race relations, leadership in the black community, the Negro intellectual and his relations with the black masses, politics or the shortcomings of public education with respect to blacks.

On Black Power

One of my speeches was given at the First Baptist Church in Spring Valley. In it I pointed out the need for ordinary people in our community to take a part in keeping our movement within the bounds of reason. I began by expressing my pleasure at being invited to speak there. I noted that as a black, a college professor, and education chairman of the Nyack branch of the NAACP, I had received a number of invitations to address various religious, civic, school and ethnic groups over the past four or five years. In each of these cases it was quite clear to me why I had been invited and what I was expected to talk about.

However, I noted that within the space of the last two weeks I had received two invitations to speak which puzzled me. The first invited me to participate in the third National Conference on Black Power to be held in Philadelphia the following week. I was puzzled because those who invited me knew my views regarding the philosophy of the black power advocates. They knew full well that I advocated sanity, reason and nonviolence in race relations. When I recalled some of the reports of what was advocated by some of the speakers at the previous year's Black Power Conference in Newark, I wondered why they would want to hear me when they could go to almost any church in Philadelphia and hear said what I would say and would hear it said better. I admitted, though, that it was encouraging to know that the planners of the conference were attempting to get a more temperate point of view expressed at this year's sessions. I was of no mind, however, to walk into an ambush, so I declined the invitation.

The second puzzling invitation was the one that I had accepted that had brought me to First Baptist to speak that night. First of all, I said, it was the first time that I had ever been called upon to speak at a Baptist church. Moreover, I pointed out, no one knew better than I that the best speakers anywhere on earth are Baptist preachers. I knew that Baptist preachers were among the best speakers that I had heard in my life. My puzzlement, then, arose from my wonder as to why the members of a Baptist church, who by definition are accustomed to hearing dynamic speakers, would invite me to address them. I allowed that program chairpersons sometimes invite speakers and find out only after the fact that these speakers are not the fiery orators that were expected. Since most of them knew me and knew that I was not such a speaker, my conclusion was that they had invited me because they really wanted to hear what I would say. I thanked them for the invitation and told them that I was flattered and humbled by it.

Speaking on the subject "The Best of Times, the Worst of Times," I began by quoting from Charles Dickens' *A Tale of Two Cities*:

> It was the best of times, it was the worst of times, it was the age of wisdom, it was the age of foolishness, it was the epoch of belief, it was the epoch of incredulity, it was the season of Light, it was the season of Darkness, it was the spring of hope, it was the winter of despair.

Though Dickens had written this in 1875 and about England, I said, I thought it was as applicable to the times in which we live here in America as if he were writing it today to apply to this country. Certainly it summarized what I wanted to say about the era in which we were living. In any case, the observations which I was about to make concerning events, people and ideas which were prevalent in America then, and which I felt made this the best of times as well as the worst of times, I made in the context of blacks and the black community.

I stated that I believed that the future of this republic was directly bound up with the ramifications of certain events and ideas related to race relations and the action or inaction of people like myself and my listeners. What was more important, I continued, was that what they and I did or failed to do about some of the issues was the key to what America would be like for our children.

It was indeed the best of times when we considered the advances we had made as a race and the benefits which we then enjoyed but which had been denied to us just a few years ago. As a teacher in, and resident of, the South during the late 1940s and the early 1950s, I had come to know at first hand the life of blacks in Mississippi and Arkansas. As a fairly frequent traveler to the South then, I saw the improvements in our lot in many of the same places that I had revisited. For example, the state employment agency in Little Rock, Arkansas, which in 1953 refused to take my application for a federal position because I was a black now had blacks assigned to it in responsible positions. Restaurants which we once could enter only as waiters and busboys now welcomed us as diners, I went on. Schools where once we could neither study nor teach now had blacks as students and as teachers. As a matter of fact, predominantly black schools and colleges in the South were complaining that white schools and colleges were pirating away their best teachers and students. Here in the North, Princeton and Yale Universities, among the oldest and best in the nation, had just appointed black men as assistant deans for the first time in their long histories. A black Baptist minister, Dr. Samuel Proctor, had been appointed a full dean at the University of Wisconsin. The Bronx Community College in New York City had a black man as its president. (Bronx Community had gotten him, I noted, by pirating him from Knoxville College, a black college in the South.) A black senator, Edward Brooke of Massachusetts, elected primarily by white voters, sat in the U.S. Senate. The cities of Cleveland, Ohio; Gary, Indiana; and Washington, D.C., had black men as their mayors. Black men and women sat as vice-presidents of banks and large corporations, as members of state legislatures, as ambassadors to foreign capitals, and one even was a member of the cabinet of the president of the United States. These achievements had come to pass because the climate for them had been created by dedicated and wise civil rights leaders and other people of good will and because the achievers were prepared for the posts when the opportunities came. I told my listeners that I didn't believe that Rap Brown, Stokely Carmichael, or any of their ilk had contributed one bit to achievements of this kind. What I was trying to say was that this best of times had not been the result of coincidence, or of the preachments of black racists, but of positive action by many rational people.

But, I went on, it was also the worst of times when one considered that the United States, a so-called civilized nation, was, in the name of freedom, bombing and burning a tiny nation of brown people half way around the world, while our brothers and sisters had been bombed to death in Sunday school by white bigots in the American South. It was indeed the worst of times when a Baptist preacher who had dedicated himself to alleviating the miserable conditions of the poor and the black was assassinated for his dedication, after a president of the United States had met the same fate, which fate in turn was later met by his brother.

As I was preparing that speech, I told my listeners, I had recalled a long forgotten conversation I had had several years before with the envoy to the United Nations from the African Republic of Togo. This young black man, barely in his thirties, educated in France, and thrust overnight into this responsible position, was naturally very much interested in the race question in this country. He therefore tried to draw me out on the subject. I recalled that he sincerely believed that there would be a bloodbath in this country, a bloodbath based on racial issues. He pointed out to me that if the bigots of this country would kill the white president of the nation, what would they do to our black leaders? I didn't need to tell the audience that the murder of Dr. Martin Luther King made me wonder if this young African, whom I considered naive, may not have had a better insight into my country, than I had at the time. I reminded them that the resistance to gun control laws in this country may be related to plans for armed attacks against black people. Reports were, I observed, that there were more than enough guns available to arm every man, woman and child in the country according to a Stanford University study. The fear of riots by black folks had, ostensibly, led white people to stockpile guns in self-defense. I suggested to them that they too probably knew of persons who owned guns in New York City and who had failed to register them under the new law. Indeed, my African friend may have been more right than I wanted to believe that he was.

In any case, I went on, it was indeed a time of foolishness because blacks were running around like wild-eyed madmen, shrieking "Black power," "Kill whitey," and "Burn baby, burn," and were really providing a justification in the minds of many for white racist power. Ironically, they were killing each other, not "whitey," and burning down their own homes, while television cameras recorded it all for posterity.

It was surely the worst of times when black men were preaching separatism and segregation with the same venom and frenzy as a Bilbo or an Eastland or any official in South Africa. It was the worst of times when blacks were stockpiling guns in the ghettoes of America for a sought-for confrontation with white people. It was the worst of times when a major political party nominated for the presidency of the United States a candidate whose first act after nomination was to pander to racists in selecting his vice-presidential running mate. When a man was elected governor of a state because of his overt acts against blacks, and another had a real chance of influencing the presidential election because his candidacy was based on a racist platform, then we were indeed in the worst of times.

I was there to tell them that night, I continued, that more of the best of times could be brought to be only by the concerted, positive action of people of good will. The worst of times most often comes to be not because of the actions of those on the side of injustice but because those on the side of right fail to speak out and to act. I quoted Marcus Aurelius Antonius, the emperor of Ancient Rome, who once said that a wrongdoer is often a man who has left something undone, not always he who has done something wrong. If Marcus Aurelius had been a Baptist preacher, I said, he would have spoken in terms of sins of omission. In any case, I pointed out, I was not convinced that most of the blacks of Watts, Detroit, Harlem, Newark and other riot-torn communities approved of the destruction and killing which their neighbors had perpetrated in these cities. Yet even we, responsible blacks, could not be heard in any great numbers condemning these events. Rather, we seemed to spend most of our time making a case for explaining away, if not justifying, these wanton acts of murder, theft and arson. It was almost as if we were afraid of what the so-called militants would do to us if we spoke out against these actions. I said to them that if we as Christian men and women did not condemn these acts, we were no better than the people in Germany in the 1930s and the 1940s who had turned their heads and refused to speak out against Hitler's attempt to exterminate the Jews. Don't you ever forget, I told them, that after the fact, history has judged such people just as guilty as those who committed the beastly acts against the Jews. When we are called to answer for our actions here on earth, how will we account for our failure to speak out against the black purveyors of hate, the looters, the burners, the killers? "What will your answer be when in judgment you are called to account for your failure to act against the unjust war waged by your country in Vietnam?" I asked them.

I did not need to tell them, I went on, that we are an oppressed people. They knew that as well as or better than I did. However, this did not give us the right to seek vengeance. The wreaking of vengeance is God's prerogative. We do a disservice to our cause, which is just, when we seek vengeance. We, the silent majority of black people, must make known the fact that we want and insist upon the rights and privileges of citizenship in this country, but we must not fail to do this within the bounds of the Christian ethic which is our heritage and indeed the heritage which is claimed by the whites who deny us our rights.

It might be well also that we remember that the 20 million or so of us cannot expect to win a violent confrontation with 180 million white Americans, who have the atom bomb, all the Sherman tanks and all the jet bombers. Even if our Christian ethic did not counsel against a violent approach, our reason, our tactical position and our minority status ought to tell us that it is unwise.

Continuing, I explained that it would be the major tragedy of the twentieth century in America for us responsible blacks to let the looters and the burners of our race cause us all to get boxed into an even more repressive society which their actions are helping to create.

I would always believe, I said, that the rioters and burners in Miami, Florida, who did their mischief during the Republican Convention there, actually caused the selection of Spiro T. Agnew of Maryland as the Republican vice-presidential candidate. Further, I believed that their riot during the convention forced Richard Nixon to pick someone who represented to the South the idea that "law and order" would rule if Nixon were elected. (To be honest

Engagement to the Cause ~ 103

I didn't think that Mr. Nixon had to be pressured too much.) In any case, Governor Agnew's statements stressing "law and order" above the establishment of justice for all at the time of the riots in Baltimore were well remembered by the black community in Maryland. Whitney Young, the executive director of the Urban League, had commented on this kind of subtle appeal to racism in his keynote address to the opening session of the 1968 Urban League Conference in New Orleans, a month before. In part, he had said,

> . . . racism is behind the code phrases being used by politicians in this election year—phrases like "crime in the streets," "law and order," "neighborhood schools," and "a man's home is his castle." All of these phrases seem so harmless—tired old cliches. But they have taken on new shades of meaning, and are now veiled appeals to the latent back lash votes.

While I was sure, I affirmed, that everyone within the sound of my voice was committed to "law and order," we should not be trapped into political positions which would make this commitment turn us into the pawns of cunning politicians who for their own racist purposes exploit our concern for order. I was sure that I would not be guilty of partisan politics in suggesting that the presidential candidacies of George Wallace of Alabama and of Lester G. Maddox of Georgia were racist appeals cloaked in an appeal for order.

As to the so-called commitment to neighborhood schools, we didn't have to go out of Rockland County to find a subtle racist campaign for the maintenance of the neighborhood school. However, it was another instance of the best of times, I noted, that the State Supreme Court had ruled against this subtle attempt to impede progress made by a citizen's group in the Nyack School District.

But getting back to Spiro Agnew, I said that it was quite clear to me that he did not represent our best interests as blacks. I thought that this was most clearly illustrated by a little-noted matter. When Governor Agnew had returned to his office in the state capital at Annapolis the Thursday before I was presenting that speech, I pointed out, he found on his desk the resignation of Dr. Gilbert Ware, a black member of his staff. Since February 1967, as program executive for human relations, Dr. Ware had been Agnew's eyes and ears in the black community. While detailed information regarding the reason for Dr. Ware's resignation was not available to me, it was apparent to me that the governor's position on race matters was the cause.

Reports were that Dr. Ware had taken issue with an attack that Governor Agnew had made upon moderate black leaders for refusing to publicly condemn Stokely Carmichael and Rap Brown. While I found Mr. Carmichael's and Mr. Brown's actions and statements to be reprehensible, and while I believed that we responsible leaders did not speak out sufficiently against them and the other extremists of our race, I did not feel that we had any obligation to do so at the request of white politicians who did not feel any compulsion to speak out against white extremists. Why, for example, didn't Spiro Agnew speak out against extremists like Senator Strom Thurmond? He had never done this. I reminded my audience that they all had heard the widely circulated report that Senator Thurmond had been given veto power by Mr. Nixon over his (Nixon's) selection of a vice-presidential running mate. Thus, I pointed out, Mr. Agnew was the vice-presidential candidate because Thurmond approved. Can you imagine, I asked my audience, Senator Thurmond approving anything or anyone that would be in our best interest?

The irony in this whole process of determining who would represent us was that the tiny minority composed of the Rap Browns, the Stokely Carmichaels and the other extremists among us have had and would have a greater influence over the selections of political candidates in this country than we would, even though there were more of us than there were of them.

I went on to suggest that the aforementioned persons had already determined, in a sense, who the Republican vice-presidential candidate was to be. Further, they were helping Governor Wallace in his campaign. My audience certainly knew as well as I did, I said, what Governor Wallace meant when he said that he would put an end to crime in the streets if he were elected. He meant that he would launch one of the most brutal, repressive attacks against black people that this country has ever seen. He had all the evidence that he needed to prove that this was necessary. There were millions of feet of news film lying around the television stations of this country showing blacks burning, looting and shooting. Let me tell you, I said, the looters and the burners had more influence on the selection of Mr. Agnew as the Republican vice-presidential candidate than Senator Brooke did, and he was the acting chairman of the nominating convention. Mr. Wallace did not have to win in order to significantly affect the lives of black people. All he had to do was hope that black idiots would continue to create the climate which provided his type of candidacy with an appeal to many people.

If they thought that I was exaggerating the potential threat of Governor Wallace, I suggested that the audience let me point out that a Louis Harris poll published on July 15, 1968, indicated that at that time Wallace could garner some 10 million votes, or 15 percent of the total. Over a month had passed since then, during which time his strength might have increased, I hypothesized. I pointed out that the June–July issue of *Crisis,* the official magazine of the NAACP, had made the following assessment of the threat posed by Mr. Wallace:

> This third party movement, essentially racist in its motivation and objectives, can become far more formidable than at first anticipated. No longer can it be dismissed as insignificant. The potential White backlash vote is strong enough to throw the election into the House of Representatives, if not to elect Governor Wallace. Nothing would mobilize this vote more effectively than a rash of racial disorders in the cities this summer. A "hot" summer this year may well mean a hotter election in November.

I went on to express the hope that I had not trod too heavily upon the sensibilities of any dedicated Republicans (or Democrats) among my listeners. In the interest of fairness I went on to say that neither party was any better than the other, in my opinion. As a matter of fact, I told them that I personally was thinking very seriously of throwing my support to Dick Gregory, the black comedian, in his write-in candidacy for the presidency of the United States. I strongly urged my listeners, if they had not already done so, to read Gregory's latest book, *Write Me In,* in which he outlined his platform and the policy he would follow if elected. In my opinion his platform was more in the interest of all people of this nation than that of any organized political party. I assured my audience that they could be sure that Dick Gregory would not make any deal with Senator Thurmond in selecting his vice-presidential running mate either.

After talking about so many things for twenty minutes or so, I asked, "What do all of these things that I have talked about have to do with you?" I hope, I said, that they suggest to you that as individuals, we blacks must become more informed and must participate in greater numbers in civic and political matters. We must make our views known and try to influence others to do the same. I pointed out that I often heard blacks say that there were not enough of us to make a difference. To these people, I said, I point out that an organized minority most often can get its views to prevail, particularly when it is opposing a less organized majority. It is a fact, for example, I said, that more people favor gun control in this country than do not. Yet the organized minority of the National Rifle Association has Congress buffaloed to the point that it is afraid to pass a federal arms control law. Also, I said, I believed that more people in this country want us to have our rights than do not, but those who do not are better organized than we are. As I had said before, I went on, we who do not condone violence outnumber those who do, but the latter group sets the tone of the way the power structure would deal with us, because we let it happen. We and those who think like us must act in order for right to prevail and for this society to become what it professed that it meant to become. That, I said, was my message to them.

I believe that I was preaching to the converted that night. I was well received. While I would not argue that it resulted from my preachments, there is a strong core of politically active blacks in Spring Valley today, and the mayor of the village is a black man.

CHAPTER 8

Alpha Comes to Rockland County

When I moved to Rockland County in 1940 the black population was small. By 1960, when I returned to the county to live and work, the non-white population had grown to 7,152 persons; by 1963 this population had grown to 8,116. Even with the growth of the county to a total population of 265,475 in the 1990 census, the population of blacks stood at only about 26,000 with 10,318 of those being of West Indian heritage. When I returned to Rockland in 1960, there was no organized presence of college-trained blacks among the 7,152 of us resident here. I decided to go about organizing a local graduate chapter of Alpha Phi Alpha Fraternity, Inc. While one member of the fraternity who lived in Rockland had been active with Alpha Gamma Lambda chapter, the graduate chapter which is located in Harlem, he agreed that an organized Alpha Phi Alpha presence in Rockland would be a good idea. Alpha Phi Alpha Fraternity, Inc., had a special significance for me when I pledged in 1948. Having just been discharged from the army after a wrenching social experience living and working with men with whom, except for our racial identity, I had nothing in common, and indeed men who were the antithesis of everything I wanted to emulate, I had a strong need to identify with black men who were achievers and who were recognized as having social grace and prominence. At New York University in 1947, I had identified the men of Alpha Phi Alpha Fraternity, Inc., as precisely the kind of men among whom I wanted to be and I joined their circle. When I returned to Rockland County in 1960 to live and teach, I wanted to replicate, in my community, the experience in brotherhood that I had enjoyed in New York City and in Little Rock.

In the fall of 1960 I looked into the feasibility of establishing a chapter of Alpha Phi Alpha Fraternity in Rockland County. I drew up a list of persons whom I knew to be members of the fraternity who lived in Rockland County. Arthur Cunningham, a composer and resident of Nyack who had attended Tappan Zee High School, had been initiated into Alpha at Fisk University in Nashville. Clarence Branch, a newcomer to Rockland, had been initiated into Alpha at Tennessee A&I State College in Nashville and was teaching science at Tappan Zee High School. Russell Sisco, a resident of Nyack, had been initiated at Morgan State College, where he had gone after graduating from Nyack High School. Walter Blount, the senior member of the Alphas in Rockland County, a graduate of Nyack High School and a prominent civic leader and official in the New York State Department of Labor, had been initiated into

Alpha at Virginia State College in Petersburg and was residing in Nyack. Robert Woods, whom I saw when I attended my first national convention of Alpha Phi Alpha Fraternity, Inc., in Atlantic City in 1948 and who joined Alpha at Florida A&M College in Tallahassee, had returned to Rockland County to practice medicine at Good Samaritan Hospital in Suffern. Albert Holland, my line brother in Eta chapter of Alpha Phi Alpha in 1948, had come to Rockland County to live in student housing which Columbia University maintained in the former Camp Shanks. He remained after graduating from Columbia University Law School and began the practice of law in New York City. Edward Vincent, who was a laboratory technician in New York City and an Alpha initiate along with Clarence Branch at Tennessee A&I State College, joined us, as did Laurence Holland, a chemist at Lederle Laboratories and Al's blood brother, who had been initiated into Alpha at Central State College in Ohio. Robert W. Jones, who had been initiated at Eta chapter in New York and was an official in the New York City real estate department, lived in Rockland County and was another who came to our attention.

I filed the appropriate documents with national headquarters and in 1961 they authorized the establishment of Eta Chi Lambda chapter at Nyack, with charter members Blount, Branch, Dunbar, A. Holland, L. Holland, Jones, Sisco and E. Vincent. Eta Chi Lambda chapter was the first black fraternity to organize in Rockland County and remains the only one chartered here. Other black fraternities have a presence here through members who reside in Rockland County but are active in chapters that are chartered in Westchester County. Black sororities, notably Alpha Kappa Alpha and Delta Sigma Theta, have chapters chartered here. Eta Chi Lambda chapter immediately began to take an active part in encouraging black males to finish high school and go to college, in consonance with the national fraternity program, "Go to High School, Go to College." The chapter began a tradition of holding an education program every year, on the third Sunday in May, at which affair we would bring in a prominent speaker and would award scholarship aid to graduating black male seniors from the various Rockland County high schools. Some of the speakers who came were Mal Goode, American Broadcasting Company's United Nations correspondent, and Samuel Pierce, who later became secretary of housing and urban development in the Reagan administration, to mention but two who also happen to be members of Alpha Phi Alpha Fraternity. The Eta Chi Lambda chapter tradition of holding an education program on the third Sunday in May began in 1954 and continues today. One current member of the chapter is a former scholarship recipient who went on to Cornell University, where he was initiated into the fraternity. Upon his return to the area as an attorney with a Wall Street law firm, Alfrado Donelson affiliated with Eta Chi Lambda; he and his father, Ulysses, constitute the only father and son members of our chapter.

 I chaired the education committee of Eta Chi Lambda chapter for over ten years and continue to be active with it after my tenure as chairman. I have served several terms as president of the group during its thirty-three years of existence. I have also been a delegate to the national convention of Alpha Phi Alpha Fraternity, Inc., for at least fifteen years. I have attended every annual national convention since 1965. These have been held in Chicago, St. Louis, Detroit, Houston, Philadelphia, Milwaukee, Denver, New Orleans, San Francisco, Miami, Atlanta, Minneapolis, Washington, Dallas, San Antonio, Baltimore, and Anaheim. I have been chairman of the election commission for the eastern region of Alpha Phi Alpha Fraternity, Inc., as well as co-chair of its national election commission. I expended considerable effort in support of Ozell Sutton in his successful campaign for election as general president of Alpha Phi Alpha and also in support of Milton Davis.

From both a civic and a professional standpoint, the two decades from 1963 to 1983 were given to my most creative thought and to my most significant activities and expressions. Moreover, they encompass my most productive years and thereby constitute the appropriate time block on which to focus my self-examination. The development of my own concept of self as a black man evolved during this period between the struggle of black people for civil rights in the 1960s and the emergence and induction into significant positions of influence of a coterie of very able young black men and women educated in the best institutions of higher education in this country. As an educator I have always been convinced that education was and is the critical factor in the making of a better life for black people. It is for that reason that I am pained by the steady decline of schools in areas where we blacks are in the majority. It is also the reason that I made an effort to be an influence in bettering schools for blacks in the Rockland County community and why I tried to lend my expertise and reputation as an educator to them in this regard.

My engagement in the cause of the betterment of the life of black people in my community was not without some professional inconvenience and philosophical reservation. I had just completed a colossal research and writing task in 1961 to earn my doctorate in French letters. I had pretensions to scholarship in the area of French letters and had carved out a niche for myself in the abstruse area of attribution of authorship, which niche I intended to exploit by churning out articles and perhaps a monograph or two proving who had written the pseudonymous "Fidus" papers in France. I would make a name for myself in the field by being on record as the scholar who had identified the hand of the writer or writers of these essays. However, just after I returned from France and moved to Rockland County to teach, Leonard Cooke, the president of the Nyack branch of the NAACP, asked me to take on the task of chairing its education committee.

At the time, I had absolutely no training in social action nor any real, organized experience in exploiting the technique. I was not strong on special pleading. Very frankly, my familiarity with the black experience was, until this time, limited to that gained from haphazard readings and from listening to and observing fellow conscripts in the 1325th Engineers in World War II. In 1944 I had already concluded that my own experience was not typical. I began a program of self-education on the subject. I undertook a reading program and committed to it all of the study time which I had planned to allocate to my attribution-of-authorship study. In effect, the focus of my professional reading and study was permanently diverted from the Fidus papers to black letters.

My reading was rather eclectic. I read, among other works, William E. B. DuBois' *Souls of Black Folks*, which he published in 1903, and several studies by or about Frantz Fanon, published in the late 1960s and early 1970s. I also read E. Franklin Frazier's *Black Bourgeoisie*, his *The Negro in the United States*, *Black Rage* by William Grier and Price Cobbs, and *The Crisis of the Negro Intellectual* by Harold Cruse. I watched more television than I had before and have since, all in the effort to get a grounding in the issues which were involved in the problem. I must have read 200 magazine articles and news reports on the subject. The Bibliography at the end of this memoir provides some insight into the black thinkers whose views I studied. This Bibliography also includes citations of selected newspaper articles, essays, and letters to the editor which influenced my thinking on many subjects.

Two things became very clear to me: (1) Some of the best minds which our race had produced had grappled with the problem for a century. (2) The proposers of the most radical solutions to our problem, solutions which many of us would dismiss as lunacy, were deadly serious, and they put their lives and liberty on the line to prove it.

I took my own moderate position. As I think about it now, I have always been cerebral in my approach to things. I had a propensity for living a life of the mind, even before I became highly educated. This may explain my ability to endure my military experience. To paraphrase William R. Hudgins, I am an inveterate optimist and I start out from the principle that I think and believe in what I do, irrespective of what others think and believe. Moreover, I don't have any compelling need to share with others what I think and believe, or to bring them around to my way of thinking. I didn't and don't believe that being born black in America made me any less able to absorb the culture and learning of this country than black Frenchmen, Englishmen, or any other nationality are able to absorb the culture and learning of their countries. It is this personal creed which makes it difficult for me to make the case for blacks who have not made the most of even the most modest opportunities available to them. Most important, I think that given the talents which I have, I have managed very well, perhaps better than some with more talent, but less self-assurance.

I am not a little amused at the fad which developed in the 1970s and persists today among some American blacks to affect African status, about which they know very little, if anything. I always supposed, though I don't know, that the colorful garments which my African-American brothers affect have significance, for example, as regards the tribe to which the wearer belongs. These neo-African wearers have less of an idea than I do, I am certain, what kinship they are affecting. Whenever I encounter one of them I play a little detection game with myself, as I wonder whether they are real Africans or the ersatz kind. When they open their mouths I usually know. I wonder, too, if francophone blacks in France concluded that I was a real francophone black, or if my accent and/or the cut of my clothes gave me away. I am no less amused by those blacks who fantasize about being descendants of African kings. Most of them do not appear to me to have inherited a regal bearing. Arrogant and self-assured as I am, I say to myself that tracing my ancestry back to Africa is likely to offer me very little opportunity to bask vicariously in reflected glory. My forebears were probably simple, honest people who were neither princes, emperors nor kings. On the other hand, even if my forebears were cannibals, I felt and feel that I am as good as anyone here in America.

From my reading I did not fail to note that E. Franklin Frazier had observed that before the Civil War leaders of the black people emerged among free blacks in the North and were associated with the movement for separate church organizations. I give great import to Frazier's further comment that it did not appear that the personality or the outlook of these men was influenced by their African background.

In the spring of 1963, at the suggestion of the branch president and in my capacity as chairman of the education committee of the Nyack branch of the NAACP, I took steps to have the branch become a catalyst in efforts to improve the performance of black students in the schools. I conferred with Professor Carl Nordstrom, a resident of South Nyack, and professor of economics at Brooklyn College and a member of the Unitarian Fellowship of Rockland County, and offered the cooperation of our branch with the proposed tutoring service being contemplated by the Fellowship. Professor Nordstrom explained that the Fellowship was in the process of establishing a pool of competent persons to staff several voluntary tutoring centers throughout the county for students who were doing poorly in reading and who were on the verge of developing into potential dropouts. I explained to Dr. Nordstrom that the Nyack NAACP branch was particularly interested in participating as regards the Nyack area. He told me that the Fellowship would welcome our participation.

Afterwards I recommended that the Nyack branch sponsor a workshop to discuss the organization of a tutoring center in Nyack for students with reading problems and that we secure Mrs. Leona Farrington of New Rochelle as a consultant to conduct this workshop. I suggested that we ask Mr. Kenneth R. MacCalman, the superintendent of the Nyack Public Schools, to send a representative to this workshop and that we ask the Unitarian Fellowship to send representatives. My recommendations were approved by the NAACP, which had earlier directed me to meet with Mr. MacCalman to discuss the state of racial balance in two of the schools in the district: the Liberty Street School and the Hilltop School. Dr. Nordstrom accompanied me and we met with Mr. MacCalman on July 30th. Mr. MacCalman was very cooperative and sought to supply all information I requested.

We explained to Mr. MacCalman that it was our understanding that black students constituted 22 percent of the student body at Hilltop School and 46 percent at Liberty Street School but that there was some question as to the recency of these figures and consequently as to their validity. He reported that these figures were established as a result of a census taken in January 1962. He then pointed out that the 46 percent figure at Liberty Street was declining significantly due to the fact that it was mainly black families that were moving from the urban renewal area and that as they transferred their children the percentage of blacks was declining. He added that on the very day of our meeting thirteen children had been transferred. Many of these families were relocating in the Central Nyack area, and would consequently be reflected in the population figures at Hilltop.

We then discussed our desire to set up a tutoring center for students who needed such help. Mr. MacCalman explained that the Nyack schools had added more personnel in the area of remedial reading in order to deal with this problem. He said, however, that he would welcome any interest and help that we could offer in this area and would lend his support to our efforts. He mentioned that he had some information concerning a volunteer center which had been organized by students at Rutgers University and said that he would look up the details of this project and pass it on to us for our information.

In my capacity as its education chairman, I recommended that Eta Chi Lambda chapter take the initiative in getting a tutoring effort going in Nyack. With the cooperation of members of the Unitarian Fellowship, and others, the tutoring center was established. Eta Chi Lambda chapter underwrote the stipend for a student from Antioch College who operated the center for credit toward his degree program. More importantly, one result of the implementation of the project was that the Nyack branch of the NAACP developed an ongoing dialogue with the Nyack School District which continues to this day. Also to be noted is the fact that the Unitarian Fellowship thereafter joined with the NAACP in subsequent petitions to the Nyack School District administration. An example of this was the instance in January of 1964 when a committee composed of Nyack NAACP members and the chairperson of the Committee for Social Justice of the Unitarian Fellowship went to Mr. MacCalman when the school budget was being prepared. We expressed our willingness to help voters in the school district understand and accept the increase which we assumed would be shown in the upcoming budget reflecting what we termed "the need for additional services and facilities which are necessary in solving the educational problems of a rapidly changing society."

Over the ensuing years we did considerable groundwork, meeting with civic groups and interested citizens (both within and outside of the Nyack NAACP branch) to develop consensus on issues and concerns affecting the black community. We would then make our views known to school officials and others, where warranted.

In the fall of 1965 I accepted appointment to the faculty at New York City Community College, a one-way one-and-one-half-hour commute from my home. I was, therefore, out of the county from early morning until evening. Consequently, I was less able to be "on the case" to the same extent that I had been when I was teaching at Nanuet High School. However, I continued to serve as lead person in education both for the Nyack NAACP and for Eta Chi Lambda chapter of Alpha Phi Alpha Fraternity. In addition, I subsequently served two terms on the Board of Trustees at Nyack Hospital, on the Board of Directors of the United Way of Rockland County, and on the Advisory Committee of the Board of Health and attended many meetings, always after a long commute and a long day.

In the spring of 1969, a group of white residents of the Nyack School District circulated a petition which called on the district to alter the then-current instructional groupings of pupils in the elementary schools of the district. The

Alpha Comes to Rockland County ~ 121

effect of this proposal, as seen by the Nyack NAACP, would have been to put black children in separate instructional groups, except for physical education, music, lunch periods and the like.

I was called upon by the branch to respond and did so with a letter to the president of the school board, which we released to the press. In this communication we observed that certain spokesmen with not a little public presence were "fronting" for known racists in advocating the changes requested in the petition. This petition, seemingly so harmless, we went on, was an appeal to latent racism. Why is it, we asked, that the petitioners did not recognize the needs of children which had not been met by the school system in the past, but which were then being attended to by the imaginative program then in effect?

Continuing, we said that we perceived a not-so-subtle attack on Dr. Albert Brinkman, the administration and the faculty of the Nyack School District as manifest in the efforts of the petitioners. We went on to take the opportunity to express our confidence in the competence of the superintendent of schools, our support of the program then in effect and our resolve to oppose efforts to change it at that time.

We justified our confidence in Dr. Brinkman by citing his performance as a school administrator in Tarrytown, where he did what we described as "the right thing, without fanfare or publicity, before pressure to do so became great." We credited him with the creation of a more democratic school system in Dobbs Ferry. Therefore, we said, we were certain that he had the competence to move the Nyack School District to the level of performance that the times demanded. We promised to use every resource at the command of the Nyack branch and the national organization of the NAACP to prevent a return to the bankrupt procedures of the past that certain urbane, subtle and genteel racists of this district were advocating. We expressed our intention to mobilize all fair-thinking residents of the district to oppose this retrogressive effort. The proposal of the petitioners was not implemented. However, Dr. Brinkman left the district for a similar position on Long Island.

Over the ensuing years, participation by blacks in the affairs of the Nyack School District increased. My own participation was a factor. Following the increase in the participation of blacks and the recruitment of black teachers, Constance Frazier, a native of Nyack, was elected to the school board in Nyack. The ultimate occurred in 1981 when Arlene Clinkscale, a black woman, was appointed superintendent of schools in Nyack, a first in the state of New York.

When I made the move to Bergen Community College I took on responsibilities which required me to be on the campus every evening. I became less active in the affairs of the Nyack NAACP and indeed in other civic activities in Rockland. When Leonard Cooke retired from the presidency of the Nyack NAACP I withdrew from the chairmanship of its education committee and was succeeded by Dr. Oscar Cohen, a Nyack resident and New York City educator. He took hold immediately and continues to give excellent and carefully considered leadership to the efforts of the Nyack branch to address the problems of minority students. I did and do continue to monitor activities and events which have to do with education in Rockland County and weigh in with an opinion from time to time. Most recently these have had to do with affairs in the Clarkstown School District, where I live.

On Another Front

I was not hesitant about expressing to the local press my views on issues pertaining to the City University where I worked. On February 23, 1973, the *Rockland Journal-News* published an editorial on open admissions in the City University of New York. The editorial raised a few issues which I felt compelled to comment upon. As chairman of one of the academic divisions of one of the CUNY community colleges which had many so-called open-admissions students, I was not without some familiarity with this program in which we had participated since its inception in 1970.

Since I felt that all educational institutions should, as a matter of course, periodically reexamine what they were doing, I didn't have any quarrel with the editorial's suggestion that the time had come to evaluate our experience with this approach to admissions. I did, however, have a real problem with the "fault" which was found with open admissions by the editorial. It suggested that open admissions takes from the job market people who might fill jobs on a technical, clerical and service plane which do not require sixteen years of academics. The argument that "creeping credentialism," the demand by employers that potential employees attend college to qualify for employment which does not presently require college training, was occurring or would occur was, I felt, a poor argument for abolishing open admissions.

Such an argument for narrowing college admissions was patent sophistry, I said. If this kind of rationale had prevailed in the past, barbers would still be pulling teeth and letting blood to cure sufferers from toothaches and boils. We would not now require formal training in dentistry or medicine of those whom we permit to attend these ailments. No one decries this, though some who now are studying dentistry or medicine might have been good barbers had they been denied admission to medical or dental schools, I argued.

I was troubled also by the fact that the editorial did not clearly identify the source of the data which led the writer to his position on the subject.

My third concern with respect to the editorial was its inference that open admissions has an adverse effect on the faculties of colleges where it has been adopted. The editorial did this by saying that the report, whatever report it was, "mentions" this adverse effect. I had not seen any reputable study which had documented any such claim either as regards the higher-education system of California, for example, where open admissions had been in effect long enough for thorough study, or as regards CUNY, where we had not yet had sufficient experience with it or the time to study the matter in any significant way. Admittedly, I had seen published articles in which CUNY professors were quoted with respect to their own feelings on the matter. However, there were testimonials to be had from some CUNY professors, some of them distinguished scholars, who were attempting to meet this challenge and who did not see it as a threat to themselves or to the university. As a matter of fact, I pointed out, a distinguished mathematician from the CUNY Graduate Center had volunteered the previous semester to teach a section of students at New York City Community College whose ability level, to be frank, was nowhere near that of his own students. One of the things that he said at the end of the semester was that he felt that he had gained something from the experience. Some of his students were quoted as making a like claim. I did not cite Professor Auslander's experience and the reaction of his students to support the claim that open admissions has not had an adverse effect on the faculty at CUNY. What I did suggest was that at least one distinguished mathematician had not been demoralized by teaching less able students than those he was accustomed to teaching and that study may show that open admissions has not adversely affected the faculty of CUNY.

I expressed the feeling that individual faculty members were reacting in one of three ways in response to the open-admissions students. Some were proceeding in much the same way as they had in the past, making no accommodations whatsoever to those students. Others were modifying their presentations and seeking new ways to get their students to learn the same information which they as teachers and scholars felt should be the outcomes from their courses. Still others were throwing up their hands and out of a misguided sense of sympathy for these students were awarding them inflated grades. I submitted that college faculties throughout the United States have been reacting to their students in much the same way since higher education began in this country.

To conclude, I did not share the fear of that eminent authority on open admissions, Vice-President Agnew, that open admissions at CUNY will result in "100,000 devalued diplomas." I said this because at CUNY the faculties of the various institutions, through Board of Higher Education by-law authorization, set the standards for degrees. At New York City Community College, where as chairman of the college-wide curriculum committee I was in a position to have a finger on the pulse of curriculum matters, there was no momentum to authorize devalued degrees. While I could not predict what other CUNY faculties would do, I didn't believe that they would authorize the awarding of degrees to all students who were admitted. I believed, I said, that those who did not meet reasonable standards would be refused degrees throughout the university.

CHAPTER 9

An Examined Life

New York City Community College

New York City Community College (NYCCC) was one of five institutes of arts and sciences which had been established by the state of New York in 1946 to offer two-year certificate programs in commerce, allied health, engineering technologies and graphic arts. It was the only one of the institutes which had been established in New York City. These institutes had been conceived to facilitate the education of returning military veterans. Thus, what had been the New York State Institute of Arts and Sciences at New York City in 1953 became the oldest community college in New York City and ultimately in the City University of New York when all of the city-funded colleges in New York City were incorporated into that university.

In 1965, when I joined the New York City Community College faculty as an assistant professor of French and coordinator of the foreign-language program, the college had recently been melded into the City University system as a community college and had had its mission redefined. There was one black chairing an academic department. He held a Ph.D. in psychology and was an associate professor and chairman of the Department of Social Science. In addition, there were three male blacks who were senior, tenured members of the faculty: two were in the Department of Social Science and one was a civil engineer in the Division of Engineering Technologies. A black woman was a tenured member of the faculty of the Dental Hygiene Department at the time I came. I recall no others in a faculty of about 300. At the time that I arrived the overwhelming majority of the college's students were white. At that time tuition at the colleges of the City University was free to matriculated students. Competition for admission was fierce and based on academic average. In 1965, the cutoff score for admission to most senior colleges in the university was a high school grade average of 83 percent. This average had to be for a standard college-preparation curriculum. Most of the students admitted to New York City Community College circa 1965 were students who didn't make the cut at Brooklyn College. Those students with averages of 82 percent or somewhat lower who wanted Brooklyn College got New York City Community College. Those whose averages were below 75 percent were out of luck. In 1970, open admissions guaranteed admission to a community college to any student who had a high school diploma, irrespective of what he or she had studied to earn that diploma. It is my opinion that most of the students who held some of us faculty members prisoner in the hotel technology department amphitheater would not have been admitted to the college before that year.

In addition to, or perhaps in spite of, becoming dean of the Division of Liberal Arts and Sciences, I enjoyed the regard of my colleagues in the faculty. I was promoted to associate professor and awarded tenure in the fall of 1968. In January of 1970 I was promoted to the rank of professor. I was elected to the faculty governance body, and as chair of its curriculum committee, I held the most sought-after and prestigious elective office in the faculty. In the spring of 1971 I was elected a delegate to the State University of New York Community College Faculty Senate. These achievements were accomplished before open enrollment propelled a wave of black students into the institution. While it is fair to say that there were faculty who were recruited to the institution more because of the intimidating militancy of black student advocacy than because of their credentials, it is my arrogant contention that my *vita* got me there despite the fact that I was black. I think that it is fair to say that this was also true of the black colleagues whom I joined there in 1965.

Under my chairmanship of the curriculum committee of the Faculty Council, a black studies proposal made its way through the committee process and I had it placed on the agenda for debate in the council. The session of the council which was scheduled to debate this proposal was probably the best-attended in the eighteen years that I spent at New York City Community College. There were more visitors there from outside the college than I had ever seen at such a meeting. I presented the proposal and recommended its adoption. I sensed that a voice vote would not have given a fair indication of the sense of the council.

The visitors, pro and con, would certainly be a factor. At a strategic moment I called for a division of the house. I have the feeling that many who would have voted against the proposal in a voice vote did not do so in the situation where their vote was recorded. In any event, the motion carried and New York City Community College had a recommendation from its faculty that a black studies program be established. The recommendation went forward to the university and it was so ordered.

Over the course of the eighteen years I was to be a member of the faculty and administration of New York City Community College I became experienced and respected and was given substantial responsibility under several administrations. Dean Milton Bassin, later president, was the chief administrator of the college when I was recruited by Dr. Israel Glasser, then head of the Division of Liberal Arts and Sciences. Dean Bassin demonstrated confidence in me almost immediately. In the spring of 1966, the state of New York, in a special program initiated by Governor Rockefeller, awarded funds to community colleges in inner cities around the state to establish centers where students who had dropped out of high school could take courses to enhance their academic skills and/or learn marketable skills. The university assigned to New York City Community College the task of organizing one of these centers in the Bedford-Stuyvesant section of Brooklyn. One day Dean Bassin telephoned me at home and told me that he wanted me to come to see him in his office. When I went there the next day, he and Dean Lester Singer, then dean of the college, took me to lunch at Gage & Tollner's, one of the finest restaurants in Brooklyn. I could not imagine what was "going down," as the students used to say. During lunch

Dean Bassin asked me to consider a change of assignment from that of administering the foreign-language program to that of founding the State University of New York Educational Opportunity Center, which was to be established in Bedford-Stuyvesant and administered by the college under the general auspices of the state. I did not have to give my answer then, but could let him know in a few days.

A few days later I told Dean Bassin that I would take on the assignment, and I spent the summer of 1966 putting together a staff, finding and leasing space and making arrangements to have it renovated to suit our purpose. Late in the summer I had a visit from some black activists from Bedford-Stuyvesant who came to advise me that they did not appreciate the fact that I was setting up a "dummy" college in their community. They threatened to put hundreds of pickets not around my "dummy college" but around the main building downtown. Having no stomach for a confrontation with them, I told Dean Bassin that I didn't think that this assignment was for me. He reluctantly consented to my request that I be reassigned to the main campus with the assignment of administering the foreign-language program. In the fall of 1966 I was back on campus with most people believing that I had merely taken a summer consulting job for the university. The Bedford-Stuyvesant black activists knew better.

Moderate versus Militant

On April 12, 1967, to be exact, I participated in a panel discussion on the subject of "Black Power" at New York City Community College. This was one of a series of discussions organized by Dean Lester Singer. This particular one had on it a member of my adjunct faculty in the Division of Liberal Arts and Sciences. At the time, he was one of the persons who was receiving national attention as a theoretician on the civil rights movement. He had been making appearances in various parts of the country giving speeches on black power and was the convener of so-called summit meetings on black power. In addition to being a Harvard Ed.D. in educational sociology, Nathan Wright was an Episcopal priest and an articulate speaker. Another member on the panel that day was the late Zephaniah Nesbitt, a community activist and a forceful advocate of black power, whatever that is or was. The panel was moderated by Singer.

I was the lone voice that afternoon that raised questions about the real meaning and substance of black power, as it was being articulated by the activists at the time. My prepared position paper indicates how strongly I took issue with my fellow panelists.

"Black Power: Pernicious Doctrine and Cruel Hoax"

In my paper, I expressed the great pleasure I felt at being there that afternoon to participate in the discussion of the important subject of black power. I observed that much had been said about black power but much that ought to have been said on this subject was being left unarticulated. It was for that reason, I said, that I welcomed the opportunity offered by that forum for me to unburden myself of what I considered to be some of these unexpressed verities. The title of my paper, "Black Power, Pernicious Doctrine and Cruel Hoax," I pointed out, was intended as a reply in kind from one of the maligned members of the black middle class to the purveyors of black power. It sought to exploit the same inflammatory technique as that used by the black power hucksters, but in this instance to evoke the thought of serious people.

The slogan "black power," I observed, was reported to have first been used by the late Richard Wright upon his return from a 1953 visit to Ghana. As a slogan in the civil rights movement, however, it got its impetus from the fiery Stokely Carmichael, of the Student Nonviolent Coordinating Committee (SNCC, or "Snick"), when he reportedly intoned it to inflame the marchers on Jackson, Mississippi, early in the summer of 1966. Adam Clayton Powell, the Harlem congressman, articulated it again to the graduating class at Howard University, also in 1966. SNCC, the Congress of Racial Equality (CORE), and other ultra-militant, impetuous persons and organizations then repeated it thereafter with demagogic fury, I noted.

I went on to observe that it was extremely difficult, if not impossible, to determine exactly what "black power" meant. Its spokesmen were not too clear on this, and consequently its meaning was largely to be understood by inference or implication from their statements. However, these statements varied depending upon when and by whom the spokesmen were questioned. It was my opinion, I said, that this was deliberate. I could not believe that Floyd McKissick, a lawyer, and Stokely Carmichael, a very bright, articulate, if irresponsible, college graduate, could not define precisely what they really meant by the term "black power." Rather, I said, I believed that a precise definition of what they meant would be construed by authorities to be an incitement to riot and violence. These men knew very well, I reasoned, that it was better for them to make statements from which one could infer what one chose. This would explain Mr. Carmichael's imprecisely stated belief that black power means that a black man ought to say and do what a man ought to do, no matter what the personal price or the social consequences. Given the right circumstances this statement may mean burn down the courthouse. Under others it may mean something else. Mr. McKissick's imprecisely stated belief that the only way to achieve meaningful change is to take power falls into the same category.

Since it was not reasonable to conclude that these two educated, presumably intelligent and unquestionably articulate men were unable to inculcate a measure of precision into their exhortations, we were forced to conclude that they were unwilling to do so, whatever might be their reasons. When they accused the press and others of misinterpreting them, it smacked not a little of begging the question. We were led, therefore, to ascribe ulterior motives to the black power pleaders.

What then of the philosophy of black power to be adduced from the utterances of Mr. Carmichael and seconded by Mr. McKissick, general counsel presumptive to the black power conspiracy? At its very best, it gave comfort to, enlisted the support of, and in general made common cause with black extremists. At its worst it exhorted its own followers to espouse the philosophy of these extremists. It was replete with heavy intimations of race hatred. It submerged the bread-and-butter issues pertinent to blacks who aspired to move into the mainstream of American society. It sought power exclusively for the black. It disavowed moderation and cooperation with whites. It sought to inflame the masses to espouse a philosophy without a program and to reject the philosophy of nonviolence and the sound program of which it was an integral part.

The public to which the black power leaders were appealing was constituted of the unlettered, disadvantaged masses of blacks who had admittedly been abused and bypassed in the distribution of the abundance of America, I went on. Mr. Carmichael and Mr. McKissick had made this clear. It was deceit of the grossest sort on their part to appeal to those unthinking unfortunates with an inflammatory slogan based on a nonprogram that flew in the face of all logic. It was sheer demagogic folly for them to admonish these people to embrace a racist philosophy which could ultimately perpetuate the very separation which blacks had so successfully fought and of which these people were the worst victims. It was stupidity of the grandest magnitude to fail to reckon with the fact that 20 million blacks in a nation of 180 million whites must work in harmony with those whites. To know this fact and to encourage the ignorant to act in a manner inconsistent with it was nothing less than criminal. When this exhortation came from an intelligent and educated man who has said, "I have never rejected violence," and who has, this fact notwithstanding, accepted and kept the chairmanship of an organization whose commitment to nonviolence is incorporated into its title, we had *prima facie* evidence of deceit. When this hypocrite was aided, abetted, encouraged and comforted by a pettifogging member of the bar heading an organization whose fealty to racial equality was enshrined in its name, the obfuscation was compounded.

This black racism which ruled out cooperation with whites and deepened the blacks' separateness served to increase the blacks' frustrations rather than to relieve them. It also robbed the civil rights movement of talented and committed whites who were fleeing from it due to the exclusionary connotations of black power. Moreover, this was not the whole story of the derogatory effects of the black power mania. This brash, rancorous philosophy, chauvinistic and intolerant of compromise, had been driving black leaders into two separate and increasingly hostile camps.

It was common knowledge, I said, that leaders of various factions of the civil rights movement who differed on means but who agreed on ends had been engaged in a struggle for some time. The black power treachery had accelerated this struggle, rendering it internecine and widening the philosophical gulf between the relatively moderate and the more militant civil rights groups. The black power delusion was an ominous threat to the unity of the civil rights movement. Its demonstrated effort to discredit the leaders of the moderate civil rights organizations advocating integration was proof of this.

At the last national convention of CORE, for example, invited black Muslim extremist speakers and other black power advocates castigated middle-class blacks as "black power brokers," presumably selling out black power in the areas of influence in which they moved. Also coming under fire were the "Dr. Thomases," who were defined as Uncle Toms with doctorates and attaché cases. (Some of us there were vulnerable on that one.) But the largest measure of the opprobrium was heaped upon "chicken-eating preachers." Read Dr. Martin Luther King. I suppose we should consider that Dr. King came off well because he could have been categorized as a "Dr. Thomas chicken-eating preacher," since he held a doctorate in addition to being a clergyman who espoused nonviolence. However, I had never seen him carry an attaché case. This may have saved him from classification in the latter species of workers of iniquity.

What was certain was that these were unwarranted attacks upon the group which had borne most of the leadership burden of the civil rights struggle and which had the technical and professional know-how that was needed to prepare other blacks to move into the fullness of American life. The extremists' obvious purpose was to classify as betrayers of the cause all leaders of the old-line civil rights organizations who counseled reason and to create a major disaffection among their followers. The effect of these attacks may have been to cause an exodus from the movement by these valuable leaders with a program, many of whom served the cause at great personal and financial sacrifice. I knew of one such case of a professional man in the movement who planned to do just that and to give full time to his practice of law. I was sure that he did not mind the loss of income which resulted from the time that he gave to the movement, nor the abuse he had received from some whites as a result of this participation. However, he refused to make a financial sacrifice and, in addition, to absorb abuse from blacks. He might get abuse for not participating, he told me, but at the same time he would be living more comfortably and providing for his family in a manner consistent with his talent.

In addition to widening an existing rift in the civil rights movement and discrediting moderate black leaders, the perpetrators of the black power hoax had done other damage. They had caused a sharp decline in financial contributions to all rights organizations. This was understandable since much financial support came to the civil rights movement from liberal whites who abhorred white racism and who at the same time understandably had no empathy for black racism or any intention to subsidize it. Thus, if the black power advocates had "won" their case in driving whites from the movement, their victory was a pyrrhic one, since they had driven away financial support not only from moderate organizations but from their own.

Another serious disservice to the civil rights movement which was not unrelated to the black power deception was the confusing of legitimate civil rights demonstrations with riots. While it must be admitted that it was not the fault of the black power mongers that the enemies of the civil rights movement tended to view demonstrations and riots as one and the same, it had to be said that rioting to the tune of cries of black power tended to give ammunition to the enemies of the movement. The black power imposture discredited the organizations that had programs and it sowed the seeds of destruction of the very organizations that had been building bridges over which the masses could one day move to full participation in American life.

There was a third very real danger that the black power folly could induce. That was a violent and general eruption in most of the black ghettoes of America. The racist demagogues who voiced the black power venom had taken the cork out of the bottle and were about to let the genie out. Once out he would not be gotten back in. In other terms, without any program for his indemnification, the purveyors of black power were rousing a somnolent black giant who had been abused. Reminding him of the abuse he had received, they offered him a draft of a heady elixir. Soon the giant would come to realize that the euphoric state produced by the elixir was only imagined and that the elixir was really a Mickey Finn. With returning sobriety would come the realization that he had been deceived and used by immoral and unscrupulous men. He would begin to give vent to his latent fury. Having nothing to lose, he would have no reason to temper his wantonness. He would wreak havoc that would make the events of the past summers in Watts, Chicago's South Side, Saint Louis, and New York's Harlem and Bedford-Stuyvesant seem like exhibitions of unusual restraint and forbearance. Through his bleary eyes he would spy the purveyors of the potion and would deal out to them a measure of his resentment and they would be consumed by the blind fury which they had generated. Unfortunately, he would bludgeon the counselors of moderation as well. All of America, black and white, would be the loser.

What then were the prospects for a return to reason in the civil rights movement? Fortunately, while the slogan "black power" was eliciting interest from many blacks, a nationwide poll had indicated that those who had come to a decision on the subject rejected this philosophy by a margin as wide as 8 to 1. Thus, it seemed that most blacks had no intention at the time of adopting the dogma of racists, or of engaging in criminal acts in the name of civil rights, or of destroying the leaders who had patiently worked for an equal sharing of the benefits of American democracy by all of the nation's citizens.

I believed that the masses of American blacks, even those who had suffered most from injustice, agreed with Dr. Martin Luther King that it was no time for romantic illusions about freedom and that it was a time for action. I believed too that they agreed with him that what was needed was a tactical program which would bring the black into the mainstream of American life as quickly as possible. What was even more important, I stated, was that the mass of American blacks appeared to be quite aware that so far, this prospect had been offered only by the program of the nonviolent movement. I concluded by saying to the audience that black power, whatever it meant, was not the solution to the race problem in America.

Suffice it to say that I was swimming against a tide. My views were not applauded or given much weight. There was not much appeal in the notion of seeking the substance behind the slogan.

"Race Related Problems"

The panelists had been privileged to study Dr. Wright's paper entitled "Race Related Problems," in preparation for this discussion. It was an excellent and well thought out document which I accepted in every respect. The only trouble with it was that it didn't deal with the ramifications of black power as it was emerging in America. Nowhere in this paper did Dr. Wright face the unsavory fact that irrespective of what the black power advocates intended, they were aggravating an already dangerous situation in race relations in this country. Upon reading it, one wondered if Dr. Wright were talking about the same movement which we heard and read about daily.

Dr. Wright said, in pious phrase, "The impetus toward Black Power is toward national fulfillment through the use of the Black's potential or power and initiative." However, nowhere did he relate this to the activities of Mr. Carmichael, for example. (As a matter of fact Mr. Carmichael did not even receive a mention in this document.) I found it hard to determine how Mr. Carmichael's activities at Miles College, at Fisk University and at Tennessee A&I University in the days just before the panel discussion were calculated to provide impetus toward national fulfillment. Dr. Wright's paper did not help me in any way to understand this. I for one thought that whatever faults these colleges may have had, as they were, they represented a better force to provide the impetus of which Dr. Wright spoke than they would when Mr. Carmichael got through with them.

Dr. Wright spoke of the stress which some militant black power advocates had recently placed on the need for the development of cooperatives by and for black people. I heartily agreed with these voices and wished that the energies of the articulate black power chiefs who commanded national attention could be channeled into such pursuits and away from the destruction of the admittedly imperfect instruments which had brought some of us, including Mr. Carmichael, to a measure of the success which we were then enjoying.

Further along in his paper Dr. Wright said, "The Black Power thrust is toward the unity of Black people for the good of the whole nation." I did not then, nor do I now, accept this, nor do or did I think that this could be demonstrated. Certainly it could not be shown in the light of the events that were occurring in the name of black power. My assessment was that not only was this thrust not in the interest of the nation but also it was not in the best interest of black people either.

Dr. Wright spoke of his belief that a creative resolution of the seemingly impossible impasse could be effected. He believed that the catalyst of black power might serve as a creative instrument for the good of America as a whole by means of developing dialogue. I believed that it could at one time have possibly so served, but that the likelihood no longer existed. Further, I believed then that dialogue needed to take place but I strongly believed that it first had to occur between the more conservative elements of the civil rights movement and the black power advocates. This, I felt, had to happen soon, before a major catastrophe was unleashed. As it turns out, the cataclysm toward which we appeared to be inexorably moving has not occurred.

I firmly agreed with Dr. Wright's admonition that instruments can and must be devised for the preservation of order while at the same time facilitating the accelerated adjustments which will characterize a world of continuing and potentially exhilarating and fulfilling change. It was incumbent upon the more moderate of us to persuade the black power leaders of this. The clock was still ticking, I believed.

Administrative Duties

I got on with the task of organizing the foreign-language program, personally recruiting excellent instructors in Spanish, French, Russian and German. I like to remember that one of the adjunct faculty members that I employed is currently the president of a community college in New Jersey. Another source of pride for me is that a second adjunct that I hired is one of only two people whose independent reading of my doctoral dissertation I can verify (my faculty advisers at NYU had read it as part of their duty). Dr. Walter Brewer of Queens College gave me a footnote in his book on Victor Cousin. Dr. Robert J. Smith of the State University of New York at Albany gave me another in his book on the *Ecole normale.* The program soon grew strong enough to be awarded departmental status, and I, as its chair, attained a vote on the powerful College Personnel and Budget Committee.

Some years later, in an effort to diversify the faculty in terms of the origins of the degrees held, the college organized a faculty recruitment team to which I was appointed. We went to the University of Chicago and to the University of California at Berkeley to recruit faculty whose degrees were from institutions other than the City University of New York, Columbia University and New York University. We interviewed some excellent candidates and ultimately appointed four or five of them, all with doctorates. They all adjusted well to the college and were reappointed at least twice. Then, along came the fiscal crisis. It became my unhappy duty to notify them that they would not be reappointed due to financial exigencies. New York City Community College made the decision not to reappoint any tenure-track faculty member who had not yet attained tenure. This was one of the most wrenching duties that I performed in the thirty-four years I have spent working in colleges. It would not have been as bad if I had not personally gone across the country and convinced these young scholars to uproot themselves to come east.

It was also my experience to chair a committee to hear charges brought against a tenured member of the faculty of New York City Community College. The professor, in the Department of Graphic Arts, was charged with insubordination and neglect of duty. My recollection is that he had requested permission and travel funds to attend a professional meeting being held in his discipline in a city in the Midwest. Funds and permission to attend had been denied. The department chairman attended the meeting and noted that the professor was there. He had absented himself from his duties without permission and had gone to the conference at his own expense. When the chairman returned, he recommended that charges be brought. His recommendation was approved; the panel was put together and I was designated to chair it.

I convened the panel to plan our strategy. Most naively we estimated that the matter would take about two weeks, what with five or six colleagues who would have to be heard and with the union wishing to weigh in on the issue. How wrong our estimate was! We spent the entire summer and part of the fall semester on the matter and concluded it early in the fall.

No sooner had we held the strategy meeting than the college received a summons to appear in the Supreme Court in Brooklyn, where the judge would look into the charge by this faculty member that we were conspiring to deny him of a property right: tenure. The president of the college and we, the members of the panel, hied ourselves to the Supreme Court on Court Street in downtown Brooklyn. The judge threw the case out, ruling that the complainant had not exhausted the remedies available to him within the college. The court would not get involved until such time as he had done so.

We began the hearing by having everyone present identify himself or herself for the record. We had a court reporter to record the proceedings for the college at its expense. Moreover, the college was required to provide the defendant with a copy of the transcript at no cost to him. The defendant had two advisers with him. One was an attorney, who happened to be an adjunct in the Department of Graphic Arts and who was well informed on the politics of the department, of the alliances and of the crossed swords there. He was a particularly nasty man, as it turned out. The defendant also had a union representative at his side. This adviser was a professor in one of the other units of CUNY. While he was not an admitted attorney, he was a graduate of Yale University Law School.

After we had introduced ourselves and I was ready to discuss what I considered to be some routine housekeeping tasks, the attorney asked if it would be proper for him to make motions at this time. Neither I nor any member of the hearing panel had any idea what this meant. I decided that the best way to find out would be to allow him to do so. The lawyer then proceeded to advise me and all of the members of the panel that we should resign. Why? Because we had disqualified ourselves by reading some scurrilous documents prejudicial to the interests of his client. The documents? The charges and specifications which the president of the college had given me with the directive to hold hearings into them. I, of course, denied this request and we proceeded for the rest of the summer, except for a week that I took off to attend a convention of my fraternity. The attorney for the defendant had so shaken us that when we broke for lunch I called the university office and requested that we have an attorney at our side. They sent us a young staff attorney from the Central Office who baby-sat us through the summer. The opposing attorney was no less obnoxious when we had an attorney on our side, but I felt better with our attorney there. In the early fall the hearings concluded, the panel deliberated and we recommended that pay increments be withheld for some years and that the professor not be eligible for promotion for several years. Eventually the professor resigned and took a position in the Midwest, working in the mint, if my memory is accurate.

I engaged in a considerable number of community college evaluations as a member of visiting teams of the Middle States Association of Schools and Colleges during my tenure at NYCCC. Some of the colleges in whose evaluations I participated were, in New Jersey, County College of Morris (twice) and Cumberland County College; in New York, Niagara County Community College and Orange County Community College; in Pennsylvania, Community College of Allegheny County; and in Maryland, Community College of Baltimore. I served on the presidential search committee which selected Herbert Sussman. I made a controversial recommendation to reorganize the departments teaching English composition and remedial writing. My recommendation was implemented after the expression of much dissatisfaction by the faculty concerned, but after approval by the chancellor. I led an effort at revision of the requirements for the degree of associate in arts which held the line against substantial efforts to water down the requirements.

I have often thought since then that I, who oppose black studies departments *per se* in community colleges, probably did more to ensure one at New York City Community College than most. I chaired the curriculum committee which superintended its honing and polishing by the faculty that was proposing it. I presented it at the council and recommended its adoption. I called for a division of the house when I felt that a voice vote was going to be problematic, undoubtedly bringing support to it from those who feared running the risk of being on the record as opposing it. I have also wondered since if there were any relationship between my expressed opposition to black studies departments and the explosion which took place in the trash receptacle across the hall from my office on the eighth floor and which brought a detachment of the New York City Police Bomb Squad to the college to investigate.

CHAPTER 10

Introspection

From a personal and a professional standpoint, my experience at New York City Community College did much to cement my fairly conservative views on most matters, including those pertaining to race. Basically, I believe that my outlook, even as an adult, has been and continues to be rooted in my experiences during childhood. I became a college teacher mainly in pursuit of a classical view of academe which was not in any way based on race. Frankly, I think that in most things I fantasized in ways that permitted me, perhaps somewhat unrealistically, to overlook the impediment of color with which I was burdened. My situation was not unlike that of the Langston Hughes character, Simple, who was given to fantasizing. Simple imagines himself to be the first black U.S. Army general in command of white troops. He proceeds to amuse himself by having them march, at his orders, back and forth along a beach until he finally gives the order to them to march into the sea. One of the other characters in the piece is heard to say, in an aside, something to the effect that Simple is crazy. The inference is not so much that a general who marches his troops into the sea is crazy as that a black who imagines himself to be a general in the U.S. Army is crazy. The thought occurred to me later that those black students who in 1969 left my office questioning, "Where do they find brothers like you to put out front?" were really inferring, "This brother thinks that he is a real dean."

The late Dr. Lester Singer, dean of instruction at New York City Community College at the time that I was chairman of the College Committee on Curriculum there, once cited the Socratic aphorism that "the unexamined life is not worth living" to support his own (Singer's) innovative curricular proposal to allow adult students credit for life experience toward the associate in arts degree. To those, myself included, who had reservations about granting academic credit for living, Singer responded that the credit would not be for having lived but for having applied appropriate academic tools to the examination of that life. Ultimately he convinced me and others of the validity of the proposal and it was approved. Consequently, when the black students at the college questioned my opposition to their proposal of a black studies department in the Division of Liberal Arts and Sciences I had a gnawing sense of guilt about my position and the validity of my rationale for it.

The real question I had to ask in my self-examination was what allowances must I as a black man make to accommodate my ethnic fellows when my convictions ran counter to the positions for which the "brothers" and the "sisters" were seeking my advocacy. It was here that the real problem lay. Often I felt that at the very least the situation called for special pleading which I could not and cannot rationalize. I remember saying to friends, after the Civil Rights Acts were passed, that the NAACP was now going to be called on to make strong arguments for weak cases. I wondered where the creative thinking was going to come from, for example, to rationalize laying blame on white people for shortcomings which are clearly our own. I was, very frankly, embarrassed by some of the pleadings which were being made by people who should themselves have been embarrassed at having to make them. I found it difficult to understand how we could or can blame white people for the deterioration of the schools in a major city like New York at the time that our children became the majority in these schools. What, for example, is the explanation for the decline in standards at the great Boys' High School in Brooklyn, which had been one of the finest academic high schools when we were not in a majority? I do not buy the argument that the white teachers stopped teaching simply because our students began to dominate the census. Why can't the generation of urban black parents who are the direct descendants of those who built, staffed, administered and made to flourish a myriad of school systems which produced civil servants, professionals and legions of good solid citizens in the segregated South do likewise in New York City? I do not have the answer and am afraid to articulate the question because I fear the answer even more.

There is an obvious corollary to the aphorism that an unexamined life is not worth living. It is that the examined life is instructive. I have asked myself what an examination of my own life would produce in the way of instruction.

Satisfactory Grade

The examination of my childhood experience sugggests to me that growing up in a family of five children, in which I was the eldest, and moving around New York State every two years did not serve me adversely in any way that I am able to identify. In fact, the fact that I have no friends who go back to my elementary school days may be an explanation for my not falling in with bad company and developing into an incorrigible youth. Being the son of Jamaican immigrant parents is, without a doubt, part of the explanation for my having developed a high degree of self-esteem. Perhaps too, the fact that I competed successfully with all comers, black or white, in the academic arena in the several communities where I lived reinforced my feeling of self-worth.

I never became a real part of any group of peers, black or white. I attended schools which were populated by and dominated by diverse white ethnics. The black communities in which I lived were comparatively small and the numbers of black classmates were miniscule. The melting pot was the dominant cultural experience that formed me. Neither black nor Jamaican culture was reinforced in any dominant way in my quotidian life in or out of the home. Academically, I did reasonably well throughout my school life and coexisted socially with students of Polish, Ukranian,

Italian and other European extractions who dominated in the schools that I attended. The academic standards of these schools tended to be uniform in conformity with New York State Education Department requirements. My melting-pot acculturation, in concert with my high-self-esteem-Jamaican-immigrant identity, tided me over my elementary school experience. By high school I had fantasized myself into the mainstream. With the exception of occasional uncomfortable days in classes led by insensitive white teachers where the subject of the lessons was the savages in Africa and the exception of the occasion of my not being allowed to learn to swim in a routine setting because of the Jim Crow policy of the YMCA in Nyack, my childhood passes my examination of it conducted now through the prism of sixty years of hindsight.

In 1967, Mother encouraged me and my brother and my sisters to visit Jamaica and to see and become familiar with the land of her and our father's birth. For me and my wife Charlene that was the start of regular visits to the "Island in the Sun." We have visited Jamaica at least once every year since. One year we went three times. We have a home in Discovery Bay and that is our winter vacation spot of choice. Before she died in 1983, Mother took us to visit with her relatives in Kingston and also to see the lighthouse in Negril, where her father had been the lighthouse keeper when she was a child. We have made friends with a number of people in Discovery Bay and feel very comfortable visiting there to relax.

Aside from the inconveniences and the frustrations which are inevitable in Third World countries, I find visiting Jamaica to be a fulfilling experience, largely because it is a country where black people are fully in charge. The natural beauty of the island and the tropical climate contribute to my enjoyment. However, it is the only black-run country to which I have been; therefore, I am not able, at first hand, to contrast it with any other black sovereign nation. But I can say that when I visit Jamaica I experience a feeling of belonging that is unlike any I have experienced elsewhere in the world. In the instances in Jamaica where I have experienced poor service or long waits for service, for instance, I have never wondered whether it was a manifestation of racial discrimination and a subtle hint that my patronage was not wanted because I am black. However, there is a type of discrimination which I have observed in Jamaica which makes me uncomfortable: class discrimination. People who in the United States would be classified as middle-class people, for instance, take subtle privileges over persons whom they consider to be of a lower social class. Persons who consider themselves to be of a lower class defer to those who are of a higher social class.

A person who comes to your home to perform a service, such as mowing your lawn, cooking or cleaning, or the like, will never come to the front door. In a public place such as a bank, an upper-class person will have no compunction whatsoever about walking to the front of a line of people to get the teller to transact his matter, ahead of others who are standing there waiting their turns. I recall an instance in which a well-dressed man came into a bank where I was the next person to be served. He walked up and stood alongside me. When the teller had finished with the person in front of me, this impeccably dressed line cutter reached in front of me and handed his papers to the teller.

He then had the gall to turn and ask me if I would lend him a pen. I was stunned. I told him I would not lend him a pen. The teller lent him one and completed his transaction ahead of mine. I have noted that employees such as that teller do not feel any responsibility to take patrons in the order in which they come. It is my observation that in Jamaica, tellers, clerks and others who serve the public defer to upper-class people and aid and abet them in disregarding any priorities which lower-class people merit by reason of their patience in waiting their turns.

In the course of my traveling between New York and Montego Bay I observed a similar discourtesy which American Airlines visited upon a group of Third World blacks and an African-American who were traveling from New York to Miami, to make connections to Haiti and to Jamaica. This race-based discourtesy occurred at American Airlines' Gate 4 at LaGuardia Airport on December 23, 1990.

I had arrived at the baggage check-in station at LaGuardia at approximately 6:15 A.M., where, as expected, I encountered a very congested environment. I got on the first-class line to check my luggage. The line moved so slowly that I was certain that I was not going to get to the counter in time to make it to the gate before departure time. Consequently, I lugged to Gate 4 both my carry-on bag and the bag which I had planned to check. When I reached Gate 4, the board announced that Flight 987 was scheduled to depart at 1 P.M., some five hours and forty-five minutes late. When I reached the counter the agent told me that the departure was indeed rescheduled for 1 P.M. but that I should be back by 11 A.M. I assured him that I had nowhere else to go and that I would be sitting right there in the waiting area. I did so. The agent left, never to grace the counter at Gate 4 again. No other person showed up at the counter to say anything to any of us sitting there waiting. (In the meantime, no aircraft had shown up either.) The cabin crew arrived, one by one, took knowing looks out the window to note the absence of an aircraft, sat down and began to talk among themselves. I waited until about ten minutes to one. I asked one of the cabin crew members if she could hazard a guess as to whether we would leave at 1 P.M., and if we did, did she think that the connection to Montego Bay, which I was assured I would be able to make in Miami, would be there. She suggested that I hurry to Gate 5, where another flight was just about to leave for Miami. I picked up my bags and scurried over to Gate 5. There, whom did I see but the genial agent who had told me that he had a connection for me to Montego Bay and who had counseled me to be back at Gate 4 by eleven.

He looked at my coupon and boarding pass and told me to hurry to the aircraft, which was about to leave. When I reached the door, the agent there said that I could not board. She said something about not being able to take the second bag. The entryway to the aircraft was closed in my very face and the aircraft left. I did so as well. I hailed a limousine, returned home, sat down at my word processor and wrote a letter to American Airlines before my anger became tempered by distance in time from the event.

I wrote to Mr. Robert L. Crandall, chairman and president of the airline, telling him that I had been going to Jamaica (on American Airlines) at least once a year, always at Christmas, for about fifteen years. I noted that I fly to other American Airlines destinations as well. I called his attention to my AAdvantage mileage to attest to this. I informed him that I had noted certain differences in the way that American Airlines treated its patrons, which differences I had long believed to be racially discriminatory, but had hesitated to articulate my feeling. Now, I said, was the time to do so. I went on, as follows.

"American Airlines did not show the courtesies and deference to its patrons who are black and whose destinations were Jamaica or Haiti that I had observed that it showed to white people everywhere. For instance, today, there were about twenty people sitting in the waiting area at Gate 4 for Flight 987. About fifteen of them were obviously Haitian and were conversing with each other in French/Creole. (One white man and his wife were sitting there. One man who might have been Hispanic was sitting there. I didn't hear him speak so I cannot be certain that he was Hispanic.) I was there too, of course. I was the only non-Haitian black there. Now, what I am telling you is that of the group sitting there, by my reckoning, all except two were minority people. My observation is that the only reason the white man and his wife were there was because they had come after the agent, who before leaving, had found other flights for all the white people who were at Gate 4." I was certain, I said, that if they had gotten there before he left they too would have been on another flight.

I pointed out to the president an example of an amenity which was extended by American Airlines to a white patron booked on Flight 987 that morning. A white couple was on line in front of me at Gate 4. The man had some kind of badge which obviously identified him as an employee with access to restricted areas. I could not see the badge because it was partly covered by his suit coat. The couple had two small cartons with them, both marked "Property of Tower Air." They were evidently attempting to retrieve some baggage she or they had checked in downstairs at the curbside baggage check. The agent extended himself by calling somewhere and describing the luggage. When the couple left I had the impression that the agent had succeeded in accomplishing what it was they wanted. I wondered to myself at the time what would have happened if I had gotten to the counter downstairs and checked my bag. Would I have had the good fortune of being able to retrieve it once I got upstairs and found out that Flight 987 was not going anywhere, as late as 12:50 P.M., and that even if it did I would not be on it? On reflection, I said to the president, I doubted it. That agent who took it upon himself to extend himself for those two white patrons was not about to extend himself to help a black one get to Montego Bay, which was probably part of his responsibility. It was unlikely that he would try to retrieve my checked luggage, which was probably not part of his responsibility.

I went on to point out that announcements were being made at other gates within hearing of those of us sitting at Gate 4 which led me to believe that adjustments were being smoothly made for American's patrons who were white and who were not trying to make connections to Haiti or to Jamaica. I pointed out emphatically that I resented the way I was treated that day by American Airlines. I didn't believe that any group of white people who were inconvenienced that day at LaGuardia Airport by American Airlines was treated as shabbily. I was traveling first class, I said, so I could not even tell myself that this treatment was because I was traveling on some kind of highly discounted fare. I could only tell myself that I was treated this way because I am black and was experiencing the contempt which American Airlines transparently manifests for its minority patrons. I promised that at another time I would recount my views on this subject as they related to American Airlines' departure area at JFK Airport, which I knew much more thoroughly than I did LaGuardia.

I concluded my letter by telling him that I was sending a copy of the letter to the co-owners of my travel agency, which was situated in one of the largest Haitian communities in New York State outside of New York City. This agency serves a very large Haitian and Jamaican clientele, I said, and did so with dignity and courtesy. I believed that American Airlines had a responsibility to serve the clients which this agency referred to it with the same courtesy and dignity with which they are referred. On that day American Airlines treated me, one of Paradise Travel's clients, and the clients of who knows how many other agencies, with something not less than racial discrimination.

I also took the opportunity to tell the president of American Airlines that I would be forwarding a complaint to the appropriate federal agency, in which I would be setting forth my view that American Airlines discriminates against minority persons in denying them routine courtesies which it extends to its white patrons. I told him that I would extend to him the courtesy of a carbon copy of my complaint concurrent with my sending it to that agency and that I was looking forward to his reply.

On April 3, 1991, I wrote to the Consumer Affairs Division of the U.S. Department of Transportation and filed a complaint against American Airlines, stating that I had filed the same complaint with the airline on December 23, 1990, but had not had a reply. I then received a letter from American Airlines dated April 4, 1991, saying that they had conducted a full investigation of my allegations, which they characterized as "most serious." They apologized for the delay of Flight 987, citing a "bird strike" to the aircraft which necessitated a wait for parts. They then went on to tell me that I must be aware that Federal Aviation Administration (FAA) regulations set limits on the size of carry-on luggage. (I have traveled enough to know that and to know that white passengers almost routinely arrive at the gate with bags that are too large for carry-on and that gate personnel take these and have them put in the baggage hold and let the passenger on.)

To make a long story short, American Airlines never addressed the issue of eighteen or so black, French-speaking patrons who sat in the lounge outside Gate 4 from 6:30 A.M. to at least 12:50 P.M. (when I left them still sitting there), who were not extended the courtesies that the white passengers who were accommodated on other flights received and who do not realize to this day what was happening at Gate 4. The Department of Transportation wrote me saying that a review of my letter indicated no violations of federal regulations, so the department could not specify any corrective action to be taken.

Oh yes, I think that American Airlines sent me a $50 certificate for my troubles. I returned it to them. My conclusion: A black first-class passenger traveling from New York to Montego Bay on American Airlines on December 23, 1990, received treatment which was substantially inferior to that received by white passengers holding inferior classes of passage, but there was no violation of federal regulations.

In the last year or so I have had occasion to consider my view of my own place in the race–ethnic group context from the perspective of the analysis which Paul Robeson, Jr. propounds in his *Paul Robeson, Jr. Speaks to America*. Robeson holds that American culture and its mass media are dominated by a monocultural "melting-pot" ideology, this in the face of the fact that America is a mosaic of cultures, with each ethnic group, in Robeson's view, deserving equal status. As Robeson sees it, the melting-pot concept limits race to color and excludes all cultural considerations. On the other hand, he argues, the mosaic, by emphasizing cultural recognition of all groups, rejects Anglo-Saxon cultural superiority. It is now time, Robeson asserts, for the "melting-pot" ideology to give way to a "mosaic" ideology. In the introduction to his book, Robeson joins the issue when he says:

> The issue of which culture we should have is linked to the issue of whose diversity we are talking about: the diversity of those who peer out at the world from the confines of the monocultural melting pot, or the diversity of those who move comfortably through the spreading multicultural mosaic.*

In my mind, I have always been one of those peering out of

---

*From Paul Robeson, Jr., *Paul Robeson, Jr. Speaks to America* (New Brunswick, N.J.: Rutgers University Press, 1993). Reprinted with permission of Paul Robeson, Jr.

the melting pot. However, I do have some reservations about that melting pot being monocultural. I see it as being multicultural in the sense that Jamaican-Americans coexisted in it along with Polish-Americans, Ukranian-Americans, and the like. In the same sense that my lunchtime confreres in Paris lumped me in with other Americans when they characterized me among *vous autres Anglo-Saxons,* I saw the melting-pot culture that I was in as being a mix of cultures that were theoretically being boiled down to some kind of amalgam. I do concede, though, that there was little comfortable movement through that mosaic by the non-white tiles which were part of it. I further concede that the new look which is being taken at the whole melting-pot concept will probably bring us to a new position, much to the disdain of Arthur Schlesinger and others.

Mediocre Grade

The examination of my life under the colors, conducted now some fifty years after the fact, yields a mediocre grade. The rating is based almost entirely on the approach which the army took in dealing with me by reason of my race. During World War II the U.S. Army had a policy of rigid racial segregation. It is my impression that little effort was made to evaluate the skills of black men and to make the best use of these skills consistent with the needs of the armed service. I can neither forgive nor forget the harsh way that the army separated draftees, strictly on the basis of their race, once they descended from the train at Camp Upton. I resented the way that we were herded into training camps in the deep South surrounded by hostile environments and subjected to the command of white officers who hated our guts. Why could the army not have commissioned some of us to command the miserable units that it activated by conscripting black men of marginal skills and turning them over to the command of white racists? However, the most heinous racist act which poisoned the quality of life for black servicemen was the practice which the army imposed in England of allowing soldiers off base there on the basis of race and date of the month. I award the army a grade of F for its personnel practices in World War II. I award myself a grade of A for surviving this ordeal without permitting myself to be embittered by it.

Outstanding Grade

My post-World War II life gets a better examination grade than does its predecessor. This is due in large part to my having enjoyed a quality of life which has been overwhelmingly satisfying, albeit a life in which I have tilted with some of the same windmills that confronted me before. On balance, though, the tilting has been on the behalf of others. I have personally enjoyed substantial benefit from my initiatives. One of the reassuring factors has been the sense that there are improvements in the quality of life available to blacks on an individual basis, determined, very frankly, by individual initiative. The possibility of pulling all of one's ethnic fellows with one through the breaches in the barrier is another matter. Perhaps that is as it should be.

CHAPTER 11

Preparing for Retirement

Preparing for retirement requires an acceptance of inevitability, just as with aging and death. To acknowledge that youth and energy must wane is a measure of our maturity.*

In the fall 1981 semester I took a one-semester sabbatical leave which was the venue for two significant personal and career decisions. These decisions went substantially beyond the scope that I had envisioned. Certainly, my purpose for seeking leave was to provide myself with the leisure and the appropriate ambiance in which to make decisions regarding my future. In my mind the one "given," that I would return

---

*From Mortimer R. Feinberg and Aaron Levenstein, "Retirement as the Pinnacle of Your Career," *Wall Street Journal,* Nov. 23, 1981. Reprinted with permission of *Wall Street Journal,* © 1981, Dow Jones & Company, Inc. All rights reserved.

to the classroom at New York City Technical College, was discarded by me in November as the result of a telephone call from Dean Mary Rothlein of the City University of New York. I reoriented my personal and professional goals.

By 1979, New York City Community College had become New York City Technical College. Emphases in the mission of the college began to harden in the technical disciplines. The role of the liberal arts and of general education in career curricula seemed to me to need more attention from the liberal-arts faculty. I had been an influence in the revision of the general-education components of many of the career curricula in the college. I wanted to carve out a niche for myself as an influence on the content of the baccalaureate programs which would surely be developed as a result of the authorization which came to the college to develop such programs. By the fall of 1980 I had decided that I wanted to return to the classroom to finish out my active career as a teacher and scholar. I refocused my interest on the "Fidus" articles which I had been studying since 1960 and in which I had developed a consuming interest in relation to the question of who the author really was. I developed some hypotheses as to his identity. I made the resolve to take on as a project of personal scholarship the unmasking of the author of this series of articles. I had published several articles and notes on the subject and in 1967 had received a research grant from the State University of New York Faculty Research Foundation to develop a computerized study of the articles to attribute authorship. Shortly after receiving the grant, I became an administrator and lost the flexibility and discretionary time which teaching faculty have and which they can devote to such projects.

I surrendered the grant and concentrated on administration for the next fourteen years. It was part of my plan to return to this research project upon my return to the classroom.

The redesignation of New York City Community College as New York City Technical College and the opportunity for me to transfer from the New York City Employees Retirement System to the New York City Teachers Retirement System in 1980 brought me a windfall of five years' credit for teaching service I had not previously been allowed. The realization that I would presumably be eligible to retire in about two years and that I must begin to plan for that stage of my life came abruptly. (Before this, I had not given any thought whatsoever to my retirement.) I realized that any activities or projects of scholarship that I could best achieve while practicing the profession of teaching would have to be undertaken forthwith if they were to be accomplished at all.

These considerations were among those which were foremost in my mind at the beginning of the 1980–1981 academic year when I informed Dr. Ursula Schwerin, then president of the college, of my wish to be relieved of the deanship of the Division of Liberal Arts and Sciences at the end of that year. I thus applied for a fellowship leave for the fall 1981 semester for the specific purpose of preparing myself to return to the teaching of French, of developing some capability to use the computer as a research tool, of developing some computer applications for my own research interests and of thinking about how I would spend the last few years of my career as a teacher. On June 30, 1981, I left the campus with the prospect of more discretionary time than I had had since the 1959–1960 academic year, which I had spent in France as a John Hay Whitney Foundation Fellow doing research for my doctoral dissertation.

During my sabbatical semester I began a daily reading program of no less than four hours per day to make myself more informed about things in general. Among the periodicals which I read with more depth and regularity than I had in years were the *New York Times,* the *Wall Street Journal, Time, Harper's,* and the North American edition of *The Gleaner,* a Jamaican weekly. I read selectively several books on subjects as diverse as current affairs, real estate, politics and finance. For the first time since 1965 I mowed my own lawn. I repaired and painted the fence along the entire side of my one-third-acre lot. I painted three rooms in my home. I savored the luxury of being at home during prime hours on weekdays. I traveled to Arkansas, to Texas and to Jamaica. In Jamaica I participated in a travel-industry inspection of more than a dozen major hotels in connection with the reentry of Jamaica into the travel industry as a major tourist destination. I participated in a conference in Birmingham, Alabama, sponsored by my church. I attended the monthly meetings of the Board of Directors of the United Way of Rockland County. (I had never attended a meeting since my appointment in 1977 because the meetings were held on weekdays in the middle of the day.) I participated in the activities of the Advisory Board of the Nyack Center of Rockland Community College, of which I was vice-chairman. I was active as a member of the Board of Trustees of my church.

In September I began a course in the use of microcomputers and in Basic computer language. (In the course with me was a former NYC Technical College staff member, then retired: Victor Timoner.) The course gave me an insight into the many applications to which a personal computer can be put, influenced my decision to purchase my own computer and shaped the specifications of the equipment I purchased.

I came to see the possible relevance to me personally of the countless applications of the microcomputer, beyond the single research project I was undertaking. I decided to commit myself to getting more than a superficial acquaintance with the computer for the purpose of solving a specific research problem. This, in turn, suggested to me the need for a microcomputer that could store more data than the capacity of the average "starter" system. I therefore purchased a computer with 32K capacity and an RC232 phone modem to allow me to tap some of the public utility data banks which permit individual subscribers to access phenomenal kinds and amounts of information. I finished the course and made the resolve to become proficient in the use of the microcomputer for application to a whole range of data processing.

In early November I received a telephone call from Dean Mary Rothlein of the Academic Affairs Office of the City University of New York. She asked me to consider coming into that office to coordinate a new program to train tenured faculty who were teaching in areas of declining student interest in order to prepare them to teach in areas of very high student demand. The areas targeted for the training turned out to be computer science/data processing and basic writing. In light of the foregoing personal goals I had set, the opportunity to participate in this venture was attractive to me. The idea of coordinating a program which had a component focusing on computer science/data processing, in which area I had just made a decision to become competent, seemed attractive enough to me to compensate for postponing the gratification of my long yearning to return to the professorial lifestyle. However, this was a difficult decision to make, because it meant giving up the discretionary time which I would have otherwise had to pursue my computer competence and research goals.

During the long period of reflection and self-analysis in which I engaged, I came to some definite conclusions about how I planned to spend the remainder of my life as an active educator. These decisions came as a result of the high level of satisfaction which I had derived over the past four months from the very ability I had to allocate my time to those things that I found personally rewarding. I realized that being able to think, on a sustained basis, early in the day when I was at peak physically and mentally, rather than at the end of a long day of commuting and work, did not have to be the luxury that it now was. I could even divert the three-hour daily commute into productive "real time," to use a term common among computer people. During the sabbatical semester I came to see and appreciate my time as a precious resource over which I had to gain and maintain personal control, not at some indefinite, future time but within a finite period which I would set by the end of that academic year.

I recalled that Dean Iraggi had once offered me a book on time management which I declined because, I said to myself, I am certainly not in the position to act on the conclusions to which I would surely be led by reading it. (Without reading it I knew that, on a theoretical basis at least, I should be delegating some things—but alas, to whom would I delegate them. Those who had been doing them had been retrenched.) Like the biblical Saul who converted suddenly to Christianity on the road to Damascus, I vowed, in the middle of my sabbatical semester, to reward myself with a permanent lifestyle which permitted me to establish my own priorities as to how I would use my own time.

I decided to retire early, supplement my pension income by taking on a few consulting projects to which I would allocate as many or as few hours as I chose, and do as priority items those other things that I found personally satisfying. By using my personal microcomputer to make my home office a "global electronic cottage," I would no longer have the three-hour daily commuting ordeal. My three-hour trips would be at my volition and at 500-mile-per-hour speeds to Montego Bay and to other such places in warm climes in midwinter to see my clients.

Winding Down

In this frame of mind, on February 1, 1982, I took on the assignment of coordinating the University Faculty Development Program with the avowal that it was a short-term commitment in my own mind and my final service as an educator. How short (or long) that commitment was to be, I thought, would be determined by the findings I would derive from a conference which I would schedule shortly with the retirement counselors of the New York City Teachers Retirement System.

At the start of the spring 1982 semester I reported to

Dean Rothlein at the Central Office of the City University of New York on East 80th Street and was assigned office space, which I shared with a professor from Brooklyn College who was on a special assignment in Dean Rothlein's office to create an online catalog of holdings of all of the branches of CUNY. Paul LeClerc, an outstanding scholar and teacher in French, was also on special assignment in this office at the time I was there. He later became president of Hunter College of CUNY and still later president of the New York Public Library.

Before I came aboard, Dean Rothlein had done some preliminary work by identifying two professors whose colleges agreed to release them from duties on their campuses to conduct lectures and seminars for the Faculty Development Program. One was a specialist in data processing from LaGuardia Community College and another, a specialist in computer science from Brooklyn College. I made arrangements for classroom space at the CUNY Graduate Center on 42nd Street. We managed to get the inaugural semester of the data processing/computer science training under way that spring. Enrollees were ten or twelve volunteers whom we had recruited and whose institutions had authorized several hours of released time from their teaching assignments each week. I visited some of the sessions, conferred with the instructors and shared my observations with Dean Rothlein.

I began to make rounds of the institutions to lay the groundwork for finding placements for these professors after they had completed the year-long program which we envisioned for them. My first visit was to Lehman College, where I met with the provost and others and discussed their staffing needs in basic English, computer science and data processing. In the discussions I had on the various campuses I began to get some feedback on the sentiment there regarding these soon-to-be-recycled professors. One department chairman asked me flatly why I thought they should take a professor who in his or her own department, over long years, had "killed" interest in his discipline and how I thought that the year of retraining that we would give such professors would be any reassurance that they would not now come in and drive their new students away. I recall reminding department chairmen that these persons whom we were retraining were not Martians or men from the moon but intelligent, highly trained men and women who were tenured colleagues in other departments of the same university. I told them that due to the current shifting of student tastes, any one of their disciplines could also experience the ebbing tides that these colleagues were experiencing. My general impression was that most departments were leery of bringing in more tenured colleagues in those tenuous times.

I continued to work with the Faculty Development Program in the fall of 1982. Meanwhile, I had consultations with the retirement counselor of the City University. In the context of the recent fiscal crisis which the City of New York had undergone, retirement had been made an unusually attractive option for persons who had more than twenty-eight years of service in the New York State and New York City pension systems, as I had. The generous interpretations of what constituted allowable city and state service enhanced the option of retirement. I made the decision to retire at the end of the 1982–1983 academic year. I exercised my option to go on terminal leave for the spring 1983 semester and to retire at the end of the leave. I gave notice to Dean Rothlein and to President Schwerin. I filed the appropriate applications in the Personnel Department at New York City Technical College. Back at the college my colleagues gave me a very warm retirement party. At the start of the spring semester of 1983 I went on terminal leave. Therein lies a tale.

CHAPTER 12

Detour to Bergen Community College

As had been my habit even when not looking for work, I continued to follow the help-wanted advertisements in the *New York Times*. January 1983, when I went on terminal leave, was no exception. As chance would have it, there was an announcement of a vacancy for an assistant dean of instruction to administer the Evening Division at Bergen Community College (BCC) in Paramus, New Jersey. The education and experience requirements were a perfect fit for me. The commute was thirty minutes each way from my driveway to my assigned parking space on campus, as against one-and-one-half hours each way, on a good day, to New York City Technical College. I applied, was chosen from among more than ninety applicants and was appointed as an assistant dean of instruction for the Evening Division, effective February 1, 1983.

My eleven years as an administrator at Bergen Community College constituted a very satisfying personal and professional experience. For nine of those years I was dean of the Evening Division and responsible for administering the adjunct faculty. I was routinely on duty from two-thirty in the afternoon until ten-thirty in the evening. Including the two summer sessions that ran back to back from the end of May, immediately after the spring semester ended in May each year, through the first week in August, I was the responsible instructional administrator for eleven months each year.

Achievements

When I took over in February of 1983, the adjunct faculty of about 300 men and women was not a very diverse group, from a racial or ethnic standpoint. By the fall of 1990 it had grown to 349 members and was a racially and ethnically representative group. Of these members, 166 (48 percent) were female, and 183 (52 percent) were male. Eleven Asians (2.3 percent), thirteen blacks (3.7 percent), and eight Hispanics (2.3 percent) constituted the thirty-two-member minority complement of the fall 1990 adjunct faculty. When I retired, the adjunct faculty had grown to more than 450 persons and, I believe, was much more representative of the ethnic diversity of Bergen County than it had been before. During my tenure we streamlined the personnel record system, the monitoring of faculty credentials and the general administration of the evening operation.

Women were very well represented in the upper administration at Bergen Community College. My impression was and is that their representation was greater than was the case at New York City Community College, though the president there was a woman when I left. In any case, during my years at Bergen, at one time or another, the college simultaneously had at least two women as division deans and two as vice-presidents, not to mention a chief librarian, a director of admissions, and a controller who were women. Blacks were less well represented in the administration than women. A black female dean had served as affirmative action officer, and had been succeeded by a white female, who was succeeded by me. For a period, a black male was the dean of counseling services.

Though I was in the college primarily during evening hours when the full-time faculty and administration had gone, my professional progress was not adversely served in any way and my experience countered the old saw that is frequently cited to the effect that those who are not constantly in the view of the senior administrators to whom they report are out of range for advancement. After serving six years under annual contracts, without faculty rank and without such service being creditable toward tenure, I was given special consideration by the president of the college which resulted in his recommending me to the Board of Trustees for exceptional treatment: reappointment at the rank of full professor with tenure. I was then advanced to the rank of associate dean. Finally, I was promoted to full dean and given the responsibilities of dean of the faculty.

Affirmative Action at Bergen Community College

From my perspective as affirmative action officer I saw Bergen Community College as being in many ways much like New York City Technical College and in some ways quite different. The proportion of black students at Bergen was considerably smaller than at New York City Technical College. At Bergen, the black students numbered 405 in 1986 and represented 3.7 percent of the enrollees. (My own sense was that black students who lived in Bergen County for the most part attended four-year colleges and that a substantial number of them routinely went away to historically black colleges and universities.) Nevertheless, I noted that, contrary to a national trend at the time toward decreasing male black college admissions, Bergen, from the fall of 1986 through the fall of 1990, maintained a black male enrollment of slightly over 1 percent, despite the increase in overall enrollment. Speaking of trends which at Bergen were contrary to the national experience, there was not a single black male or female that I can recall who taught, coached or was in any way professionally associated with the health and physical education discipline at Bergen Community College, either full- or part-time.

In the fall of 1990 there were 515 black students registered at Bergen, constituting 4.1 percent of the student body. By the time I had left New York City Technical College in 1983, my sense was that the student population was at least 50 percent black. I noted recently that the institution is now listed as a majority black institution in at least one national higher-education statistical source. My feeling is that at Bergen the heterogeneous groups of students, taken together, were significant contributors to the diversity of the critical mass of students which made the college representative of the world into which these students would go after their experience there. My feeling about the critical mass of students at New York City Technical College is that the lack of heterogeneity adversely affects the ability of that college to create an environment where the interaction of diverse cultures is optimized.

Faculty Unions

Another striking difference that I detected between the two institutions has to do with the faculty labor-relations cultures. Admittedly, my assessment of each of these labor-relations cultures is based on observations made without having been witness to the preceding events which produced the *faits accomplis* which I assess. In a word, I arrived at New York City Community College just before collective bargaining was imposed by state law. All of the roiling which led up to this had ended. (The referendum on this issue took place while I was there. I voted against collective bargaining, but a majority of the faculty in the City University voted for it and it was implemented.) The point is that the impression that I have of the labor-relations culture of New York City Community College is based totally on impressions which I drew from what was said to me by colleagues, both on the faculty side and on the administration side, when I joined that college nineteen years into its history. Likewise, the impression that I have of the labor-relations culture of Bergen Community College is based totally on my observations and discussions with faculty and administrators after I joined that college thirteen years into its history. (It is to be observed that the year that I joined New York City Technical College, Bergen Community College was being founded.)

As I saw it, the influence and posture of the faculty union at Bergen Community College was an interesting study in contrast to that at New York City Technical College. The union at the latter institution was very strong and was led by Dr. Israel Kugler, one of the pioneers in organizing college faculty long before collective bargaining became respectable and mandated by law. An NYU Ph.D., Kugler was an articulate, knowledgeable and experienced labor union negotiator. He was a consummate performer in the classroom and commanded respect as an academic. He had experience in the rough-and-tumble New York labor movement outside academe. He drove a hard bargain and lived by it for its term. The college lived by the bargain as well. I don't have any recollection that there was ever any impression, either on the part of the administration of New York City Technical College or on the part of the Professional Staff Congress, its union, that there was any prospect of renegotiating any part of the contract during its term.

From my perspective, the union at Bergen Community College suffered from comparison with that at New York City Technical College. At least one of the top leaders of the union at Bergen Community College gave me the impression that he had a less-than-assured feeling about his competence in the classroom. I say this because when he was put on a list of persons whose classes I was to visit to conduct a performance evaluation, he forthwith successfully negotiated with my supervisor for a cancellation of this visit. I, of course, complied with the directive to cancel which I received from her. I never got inside his classroom for a performance evaluation. I would simply add here that no union official, or any other faculty person at New York City Technical College, ever negotiated an exemption from a scheduled performance evaluation visit by me in the eighteen years that I was there. The only instance in which I experienced this over my career is the one cited here. One night, however, I did get a request, relayed by him, to come to his classroom at once. When I got there I found him in a running argument with a student about some pedagogical matter. He wanted me to remove the student from the class at once. This was something that I did not have the authority to do. What I did do was ask the student to come with me to my office to discuss the matter. He did so. To make a long story short, the student was a six-foot-tall, ex-Marine, Vietnam veteran. He said that he had questioned the instructor about a matter they had been discussing in the class and that the instructor could not give a satisfactory answer and took exception to his (the student's) insistence in questioning. The student said that what bothered him even more was the instructor's "John Wayne–type belligerence." He said that as an ex-Marine it was all he could do not to respond in kind. I convinced the student that he should not return to class that night and assured him that I would (and did) make an appointment for him to meet with the dean of the Division of Natural Science and Mathematics to discuss the matter.

My observation is that the union at New York City Technical College more resembled an association of professionals than did its counterpart at Bergen. The Professional Staff Congress, as it was known, arrived at agreements, signed them, and, as far as I could see, lived up to them. At Bergen, on the other hand, I always had the feeling that any issue which arose during the life of a contract was fair game for renegotiation then and there by the Bergen Community College Faculty Association. In light of the fact that it had managed to accomplish this more than once, I never really felt assured that any policy could be implemented with any assurance, even though it had been agreed to by the union in the contract currently in force. Thus it is, though I don't think I ever let on to this, that I always felt a little intimidated by the overbearing manner of the union leadership at Bergen Community College. I shall never forget the feeling of embarrassment that I experienced in a meeting with outsiders that I attended, very early in my tenure at Bergen, in which one of the union leaders conducted himself in a manner which bespoke a lack of rudimentary courtesy, not to mention a lack of professionalism. His behavior in intruding his overbearing union posture into the meeting would have been more appropriate in a negotiating setting than it was in a meeting in which the agenda dealt with academic matters. I wonder to this day what those outsiders thought about the college as they observed this man's behavior. I never overcame my embarrassment at his behavior, but I learned to live with it. The union at this college resembled more an industrial union of the 1930s than it did a professional association of college faculty.

My impression is that the union at Bergen felt that it had had substantial influence in driving the immediate past president away from the college. Having serious, substantial differences with the man, the union had indeed lobbied the Board of Trustees and others to get him out. After he left, it seemed to me, the union wanted to keep fresh in everyone's mind its perceived impression of its influence. This resulted in a persistent, uncalled-for truculence which the union intruded into situations where it was not warranted. In my view there are two factors which explain this phenomenon. Again I see the situation in the context of my observations of New York City Technical College.

New York City Technical College had a history of about twenty years of operation before legally mandated collective bargaining came into the picture. Those who were attempting to organize a union there could not meet on campus. From the horror stories I heard from some of them, they were seen by the administration as subversive persons. In any event, for twenty years the administrators ran the college with a strong hand, with little interference from an organized union. On the other hand, the administrators at Bergen Community College did not have this luxury in 1965 when they organized the college. The union was there from day one, so to speak. The administration at Bergen never had the opportunity to put its imprimatur on the institution. The union quite obviously "hit the ground running." It took both the faculty and the administration captive.

Over the twenty-five years of the life of the college, the union maintained the same leadership! Over that period, the officers of the Faculty Senate and the leadership of the union were one and the same. The administration negotiated with the union in any matter of governance which arose. This persisted until about 1990, when I observed what I characterize as a philosophical line which the president drew in the academic sand. I see it now as a watershed event in the presidency of Dr. Lopez-Isa. I do not recall exactly how it happened, nor indeed if I ever knew. What came to be understood by the union was that its gratuitous, unheralded, and unscheduled incursions on the president's office would no longer be countenanced. Meetings would be held at the times and on the agendas called for in the union contract. The difference in the deportment of the union leadership changed noticeably in this regard. I do not recall, for instance, any interruptions thereafter by union officers of meetings in the instructional deans group. A year or so after that Dr. Lopez-Isa announced to a stunned faculty that he was not going to seek another contract as president of the college when his current contract expired at the end of the 1994–1995 academic year. For the next two years it was my observation that President Lopez-Isa had set a course to rectify all of those things which he felt needed correcting. He appeared to really enjoy at least the last three years that I was there. I enjoyed them too, because when he called for my advice in my capacity as affirmative action officer he authorized me to implement recommendations which I am sure leveled the playing field for minority applicants for positions in the support staff of the college. Before I left, my recommendations had already produced at least one appointment which would not have been achieved had we not implemented them.

Getting back to the academic side of things, it was my observation that the union began to take harder positions in its bailiwick. So much so that, reaching the height of arrogance, the senate (read union) refused to provide to the president the official minutes which he requested concerning certain actions taken by it and on which he was called upon to act. The president took the position that he would wait until he received the information he had requested before taking action on several matters. He began to seek advice from other sources on matters on which advice normally came from the senate. Most notably, these other sources were the divisional deans, myself, and the members of his cabinet. This standoff was still in place when I left.

The extent of abdication of its prerogatives by the faculty to the union at Bergen Community College was a source of no little amazement to me. Particularly so was the collaboration by some very able people. My observation was that there were some weak faculty members who understandably were knee-jerk unionists. However, there were some exceptionally able faculty members whose achievement and credentials had given them status as experienced, competent, tenured senior professors, but who manifested as little independence from the union as did their marginal colleagues. I recall one faculty member whose credentials, performance and judgment I respect profoundly, whose lockstep, knee-jerk unionism parallels that of those whose membership on that faculty I deem to be explained solely by the fact that those who should have done something about their presence did not do so in a timely manner. They were, and remain, grateful and loyal union members. I don't blame them. As for the able ones, I don't understand why they feel so beholden to the union and why they tolerate the climate it has created. On leaving this subject I must say that tenure has outlived its usefulness. I believe that with collective bargaining we no longer need a tenure system. Able, tenured faculty members don't buck the union. Incompetent ones don't either. Why do we need tenure? My conclusion was that it is a waste of resources.

The intersecting of collective bargaining and tenure at Bergen Community College calls to mind the comment of an early twentieth-century president of one of the selective men's colleges in New England. He defined "tenure" as a device created by the devil to introduce sloth into the world. My observation is that the tenure-created sloth, in tandem with collective bargaining, constitutes the "hounds of hell" that bedevil the paths of administrators in the groves of academe. I am also reminded of the comment of H. L. Mencken, who said that all professions are conspiracies against laymen. At Bergen Community College the faculty association is a conspiracy against the profession.

Despite the foregoing, Bergen Community College appeared to me to be what I would call a "threshold" institution with great potential for the future. In my view, the strength of this institution is in its administrative organization and staffing. This was, as I see it, a legacy of the administration of the immediate past president of the institution. That legacy is an organization in which the academic divisions headed by deans subsume the functions which in other institutions are performed by elected department chairpersons. I shudder to think what the state of academic affairs would be in this college if between 1983 and 1993, elected chairpersons, for example, the union designees, had

had the whip hand on the curricular life of the several divisions. Since academic affairs have been managed by strong deans, serving at the pleasure of the president and under the direction of an academic vice-president, these affairs have gone on remarkably well, given the circumstances. I draw an analogy between the comment which was made about the civil service system of France right after World War II, when changes in government were legion. It was said that it didn't matter who was the premier, because the civil service held things together. The academic program at Bergen Community College was held together by the academic deans under the leadership of the president and the deans/vice-presidents of academic affairs, the Bergen Community College Faculty Association notwithstanding.

While I am the first to acknowledge that there is a whole range of support services alongside the Office of Academic Affairs that contribute to the success of an institution, I feel that the Office of the President and that of Academic Affairs played a major role in the successes of Bergen Community College in the years between 1983 and 1994. While these years are those that parallel my service at Bergen, I do not mean to imply that my role was pivotal. I say only that I observed at first hand the administration of the college and was part of it.

At New York City Technical College I was an associate dean in charge of the Division of Liberal Arts and Sciences. I was therefore part of the senior administration and in a position to observe its workings. As a matter of fact, after being at Bergen for less than one year I came to the conclusion that my experience at NYC Tech was such that I could use it as a referent for almost any activity, issue or situation in which I found myself. I felt quite comfortable in this context. In meetings where we were deliberating various issues, similar issues which I had experienced would come up and I would cite colleagues at NYC Tech with whom I had interacted and experiences from which I had profited. I quoted the late Dr. Thomas Shaw, my predecessor as dean of liberal arts, on the subject of evaluating applicants for promotion, the late Lester Singer on life experience as part of one's education, and President Leon Goldstein, now of Kingsborough Community College, who once said that given what he has learned on the job, he would not now hire himself for his job. (In 1986 or 1987, the chancellor's office at the City University invited me to serve on a team to evaluate President Goldstein's performance as president of Kingsborough Community College. I, along with the other members of the team, was highly impressed with what he had accomplished there. I would hire him for his job, even if he would not hire himself.) In this context I assessed the two administrators to whom I reported at Bergen Community College.

Dr. Jose Lopez-Isa, president of the college, was a strong academic. A refugee from Castro's Cuba, he had been a professor at Dutchess Community College in upstate New York before coming to Bergen to organize the Department of Foreign Languages when the institution was founded. Elevated to the presidency of Bergen Community College on the departure of then-president Alban Reid, he had been president for a year or so when I was appointed. He had a great interest in international education and had contacts throughout Latin America and Spain. His interests and contacts resulted in many foreign students coming to

Bergen Community College. I attribute considerable credit to him personally for the level of heterogeneity that existed in the student body toward the end of his administration. The resultant diversity of the critical mass of students which this made is a tribute to his initiative.

Dr. Lopez-Isa took a classical view of academe, much as I do. He believed that faculty should make decisions by collegial consensus in a democratic setting. He was particularly crushed by the faculty union's characterization of him as a threat to collegiality. One of the most moving arguments I ever heard him make was in response to the union's portrayal of him as a tyrant. He stated that he would match his record of dealing with tyrants with that of anyone in the college. I believe that from that point on, the union knew that it was not dealing with a pushover.

I once saw a film on the Wildlife Channel in which a porcupine was defending itself against a lion in a veritable cat-and-mouse scenario. The lion either stood over the porcupine, walked around it, or walked away feigning indifference, only to return to repeat the process. The porcupine kept turning to aim its quills toward the lion to hold it at bay. Ultimately, the lion's attention was distracted by a summons from its fellow lions whose own safety was being threatened by some other predatory beasts. The lion left the porcupine and joined in solidarity with its fellows against a common threat. When I left Bergen Community College, the Board of Trustees was putting together a process for conducting a search for a president to succeed Dr. Lopez-Isa. The union was beginning to perceive a threat to its influence being built into the process and was turning its attention to that.

Toward the end of my tenure at Bergen, Dr. Lopez-Isa made the decision, for cause, to replace his vice-president/dean for academic affairs. He selected Roanne Angiello, a bright, young, energetic woman who is impressive in her ability to think on her feet and who is a strong leader. She had had experience as a professor and some academic leadership experience in community colleges in Texas and in Virginia before coming to Bergen, where she was dean of the Division of Business Technologies prior to becoming dean for academic affairs, and then vice-president. I had become aware of and impressed by her administrative ability when I served on a search committee screening for a deanship in the Office of the Dean of Faculty. I became more impressed with her when she went into that office and I reported to her. I found her to be a perfect complement to Dr. Lopez-Isa in the latter years of his administration, when he was on the course I describe as rectifying things that needed correcting. When she came down to my office one night to ask me to consider coming into the Office of Academic Affairs I was as stunned as I was flattered. I certainly had not the remotest interest in moving up any further on the career ladder. As a matter of fact, the major reason I was still working was that I thought I owed it to the college to give more service after so recently being awarded faculty rank and tenure. However, I had begun to see that some of the things that I wanted to accomplish as dean of faculty would take longer than the period that I planned to continue working. Therefore, I took the position largely because of the admiration I had for Roanne Angiello's intellect and integrity and to a lesser degree because I also thought that I would be able to do some hard things that needed to be done that were better done by someone who was on the way out rather than on the way up. I knew that I would enjoy collaborating with Dr. Lopez-Isa and would enjoy ending my career working on some things on that level. I thus became one of the "porcupine quills." I think that I accomplished some things that advanced Dr. Lopez-Isa's administration and routinized some procedures in the Office of the Vice-President for Academic Affairs during Roanne Angiello's watch.

CHAPTER 13

Rewriting History

I had curtailed my civic activities sharply upon taking the appointment at Bergen Community College in 1983. This was because my workday at Bergen began at 2:30 P.M. and ended at 10:30 P.M. The activities in which I had engaged in my community for the previous fifteen years or so had been in the evenings. Since my work now required me to be out of the county every evening, I withdrew from these activities. However, I took on one new activity as a member of the Board of Visitors at the Rockland Psychiatric Center. Walter Blount, a longtime member of the board, had proposed my name and I was appointed by Governor Cuomo. This board held its regular meetings during the day, so there was no conflict with my work schedule. I continued to keep up with events and issues which were current in Rockland County.

Face to Face with Bias

In the early spring of 1990 I read in the *Rockland Journal-News* that a member of the local school board, Mr. Joseph Pantano, had said that history should not be rewritten to include the contributions of minority persons. Since school elections were about a year away I wanted to hear this gentleman out on this issue, and I knew that others would as well. I wrote a letter to the editor outlining my position on the issue. I telephoned Mr. Pantano at his home, told him that I was black and that I had read that he opposed rewriting history in light of new findings and asked if the quotation was an accurate reflection of his view. In the virtual monologue which ensued, my representative on the Board of Education of the Clarkstown School District gave me an insight into his views on this subject.

He explained that in talking with the reporter, he had reacted to a suggestion of a group that wanted to include in the curriculum of New York State a reference to a Mr. Campos, a Puerto Rican who had led a group that wanted to assassinate President Truman. I told Mr. Pantano that I did not have that type of information in mind when I wrote my reaction piece to the attribution to him by reporter Chang of the opinion that history should not be rewritten to include the contributions of minority persons. His response to me was that he had questions regarding the rewriting of history, even to meet the objections of people other than blacks. He would have a problem with rewriting history to show that Mussolini was able to run the trains on time but not include the assessment that he was a bad man. I told him that I supported the rewriting of history to include contributions of groups which documentation suggested had been overlooked. He then talked at great length about his view that we are Americans first and members of other groups afterward. He said that he was of Italian heritage, but that he was an American. He said he did not know where my parents came from. Not feeling that to be relevant I did not tell him. Mr. Pantano went on to talk about a class that he had visited that day, and commented on the fact that the students were performing below level. He said that it was more important that students be brought to level in reading and mathematics than that money be spent rewriting history. In the course of our conversation I told him that I was quite familiar with the curriculum of the state of New York, having received my elementary and secondary education in the public schools in the counties of Nassau, Westchester, Columbia, Orange and Rockland.

Mr. Pantano pointed out for my edification, as if I were not painfully aware, that there were few blacks in Clarkstown and that the schools had more trouble with white students than with black. I concurred with his statement that there were fewer blacks than whites and that it was quite natural that there would be fewer problems with blacks. I restated my view that when the evidence is present we should rewrite history to include the contributions of minorities. Mr. Pantano continued to maintain that we might "add" the contributions of minority persons who do not advocate the assassination of elected officials and who are appropriate role models, and that this certainly would not include Mr. Campos. However, Mr. Pantano informed me, we may find it difficult, if not impossible, to find contributions made by people from places such as Liechtenstein to include in our history. "Liechtenstein is a very small country, you know," he said, as if I didn't know that. "We might find that none of them had made any contribution to the history of this nation." We ended our conversation amicably with each maintaining his point of view.

 The following spring I wrote to my elected representative on the school board. I reminded him that I was the black resident of the Clarkstown School District who had taken issue with him a year ago regarding his view that history should not be updated, particularly as it relates to the contributions of minority people. I asked if he had modified his views on this subject over the past year. I took the opportunity to include a press release which our congressman, Mr. Gilman, had issued on the occasion of Black History Month the previous year. I pointed out that while I was not a member of any political party, and therefore had no partisan axe to grind in citing Mr. Gilman's position on the appropriateness of having the contributions of black citizens chronicled in the history of this nation, I was personally pleased to forward a copy of this release to him. I went on to state that I had been a classmate of Mr. Gilman in high school and had been a participant in an extracurricular activity in which he was the leader.

 I also enclosed a copy of an essay written by Albert Shanker, president of the American Federation of Teachers, for the observance of Black History Month that year. I revealed to Mr. Pantano that while as an educational administrator I had not always agreed with Mr. Shanker, I was in total agreement with his views on the subject of the contributions of black people to the history of the United

States of America and the need to update history to reflect them. I expressed great pleasure at sharing these with him and said that I looked forward to his early reply as to whether or not he had modified his views on the matter of the updating of history to reflect overlooked or bypassed events and contributors. Regrettably, Mr. Pantano did not favor me with a reply. The following spring he was defeated in his bid for reelection. I do not take much credit for this, though, because the gentleman put his foot in his mouth on several issues and the electorate of the school district turned him out.

Epilogue

Thank you for sharing my recollections, reflections and impressions garnered from a forty-five-year working life in a career that rewarded me richly. I suspect that many of you are among my peers who awarded me tenure everywhere I worked when it was within your power to do so and who promoted me to the loftiest rank that was in your purview to grant. I also thank those of you who were my students and who gave me your attention and approbation. I cherish highly the Outstanding Teacher Award which those of you in the Alumni Association of New York City Community College gave me in 1973. To have students who sat in my classes no less than five years before not only remember me but, more significantly, write my name in and propose me for such an award is humbling. To have colleagues who sought my advice, and in some instances followed it, has been gratifying. To paraphrase William

Henry Channing, you made it possible for me "to live content with small means; to seek elegance rather than luxury, and refinement rather than fashion; to be worthy, not respectable, and wealthy not rich; to study hard, think quietly, talk gently, act frankly; to listen to stars and birds, to babes and sages, with open heart; to bear all cheerfully, do all bravely, await occasions, hurry never. In a word, to let the spiritual, unbidden and unconscious, grow up through the common." Again with apologies to Channing, this has been my symphony.

Notes

Chapter 1

The Harold Faber article in the *New York Times* substantially refreshed my recollections of the city of Hudson, New York, from 1935 to 1938. The article, which was published three years after I had written this chapter touching on my memories of living there, caused me to think again about events which occurred in those years, and to reorient my recollections in the context of the new Hudson which emerged in the Faber piece. Some things which I had recalled, but had not mentioned because they did not seem significant at the time, took on real significance in the context of Faber's revelations. For example, before reading this article I had recalled the activity which I inadvertently observed from the gangway window, but did not mention it in the first draft of this chapter. I recalled the men in the house next door, their houseguest and the like, but did not include them in the first draft. I remembered, of course, my encounter with the slingshot-propelled chestnut and also Mother's near-fatal New Year's Eve shooting. I had not mentioned them in the first draft either. "Hudson Casts New Light on Its Red-Light Past" cast a new light on my Hudson experience. The events that I had passed over were a significant part of the Hudson which was revealed by the "new light." The only reservation that I retained was that of not mentioning the name of the man who fired the shotgun which hit Mother or that of the boy who shot me in the eye, though I remember both.

I have established to my own satisfaction that the second house from the right in the picture illustrating Faber's article is indeed 215 Columbia Street. Several intriguing questions remain for me, which I will probably pursue when other pressing research obligations are discharged. For example, Faber tells us that "in Hudson in the 1930's, there were 15 brothels on Diamond Street, now Columbia Street." All of the brothels identified by Bruce Hall in his book *Diamond Street* were in the 300 block. Were there ever any in the 200 block? Were there any in the 1935–1938 era? In which houses were they? Who owned 215 Columbia Street in the 1935–1938 era? When did Mae Gordon come into possession of it? Did she ever conduct any of her nefarious activities in it? When? (215 Columbia Street was clean from 1935 to 1938.) How did the house next to the gangway figure in the scheme of things?

It seemed appropriate for me to try to flesh out my recollections of our life at 215 Columbia Street by discussing the matter with Louise, Ida and Catherine. I did so at a family gathering at Ida's home on November 26, 1994. I prepared the following composite from that discussion. To respect their privacy, I have not used the surnames of any of the persons involved in these recollections.

Collage of Reflections

The others remember that there was a porch on our house at 215 Columbia Street and that it had a green awning that Mother kept down. The house in the picture in the Faber article does not have a porch as remembered by the others, but only a stoop. The others also remember that Mother kept the shades drawn on the windows on the gangway side of the house.

Solid Citizens of the 200 Block of Columbia Street

We all remember that the P. family lived in the house next to us on the 3rd Street side and that this house had a vacant pool room in it on the street floor. We all remember that the W. family (a black family) lived a few doors up the street on our side and that the children's names were Selma, Naomi, Arthur and Chester. I remember going to their house to listen to Joe Louis fights on the radio. We had no radio. We all remember a house across the street occupied by an old man, Tommy D., and his sister, Mary D. (whites). I remember how irritated Mary D. would get at children roller skating on the sidewalk past her house. We all remember W.'s Saloon directly across the street, as we do Hollenbeck's coal yard, also across the street. We all remember a black family named S. who lived across the street and a few doors up toward 3rd Street, in which the mother had died and the father was raising the children (Annie, Esther, Elijah and Andrew). Catherine considered Esther to be a good friend and remembers that they played jacks together. She remembers also that Esther always had a brown bag of candy which she shared generously. The first person that I can remember as Jewish while I was growing up was a girl who used to play with Catherine, Ida and Louise and who lived across the street and up the block toward 3rd Street. I recall distinctly that she was playing with them one day and writing on the sidewalk with chalk, remembered that it was a Jewish holy day when she should not write, dropped the chalk and ran home horrified. They remember her as Clara E.

Catherine remembers Otto, the son of the saloon proprietor, being in her class in school. We all remember Jenny C., who lived in a house a few doors down the street (toward 2nd Street) on the other side and who played with Catherine, Ida and Louise.

Catherine remembers fighting Joey C. (not related to Jenny C.) for something he did to Louise. None of us remembers where Joey lived, or even if he lived on Columbia Street.

We all remember Mr. J., a member of the church trustee board who lived on our block close to the corner of 3rd Street. We all remember Dr. P., a black physician who had his office in a building on our side of the street near to 2nd Street. The others remember that his office was in the same building with a bakery, where we used to buy pumpernickel bread, hot from the oven, at a nickel a loaf.

On the Other Side of the Gangway

We all remember a large warehouse for a brewery which was two doors down the street, next to the house on the other side of the gangway, where trucks brought empty beer barrels. We all remember this site as the "Big Yard" and recall that men played bocce there. Catherine remembers a somewhat sickish smell of freshly baked bread mixed with the smell of beer wafting from the Big Yard, where the empty kegs of beer were stored.

We all remember that one of the men in the house across the gangway was named, or nicknamed, B. The others remember that he had a brand-new automobile and that some person or persons had let the air out of his tires one night and that he announced that he would hereafter be in the window of the house with his rifle and would shoot anyone whom he saw near his car. Catherine remembers Daddy trying to get B. to come to church, but doesn't recall that he succeeded.

Chapter 2

The only official document of the 1325th Engineers which I have been able to find among my army papers is a copy of an extract from General Orders No. 3, under the date of 10 July 1945. I have reproduced it below. Some explanations and comments regarding this document are warranted at this point.

On July 10, 1945, when these orders were promulgated, the regiment was either in the staging area in southern France preparing for embarkation or on board the ship on the way to the Western Pacific theater of operations. The extract reproduced here is of that portion of the orders which applied to members of Company F. It was as a member of Company F that a copy of it came into my possession.

HEADQUARTERS
1325TH ENGINEER GENERAL SERVICE REGIMENT
APO 513   U. S. ARMY GENERAL ORDERS: 10 July 1945

NO . . . . 3:   EXTRACT

8. VOCO is hereby confirmed and made a matter of record for the awarding of the Soldiers' Good Conduct Medal to the following named Enlisted Men of this Regiment. The men, awarded on the dates indicated have demonstrated fidelity through faithful and exact performance of duty, efficiency through capacity to produce desired results and whose behavior has been such as to deserve emulation:

Company "F"

Rank	Name	ASN	Date Awarded
S/Sgt	Elwood, James	383261886	17 Aug 44
S/Sgt	Bynton, Jr. Willard	34908970	16 Jan 45
S/Sgt	Nicholas, Eddie W	34046184	17 Aug 44
Sgt	Bowles, Thomas H	33752677	2 Feb 45
Sgt	Hawley, Willie J	33853513	16 Jan 45
Sgt	Oliphant, John	33811223	16 Jan 45
Sgt	Sherrill, Jr. Rufus	34906760	16 Jan 45
Tec 4	Dunbar, Harry	42066350	16 Jan 45
Tec 4	Moss, Monroe	38601497	16 Jan 45
Tec 4	Ricks, Jr. Howard	42082682	2 Feb 45
Cpl	Boone, Winfred H	33853622	16 Jan 45
Cpl	Heno, Albert J	38502819	16 Jan 45
Tec 5	Anderson, Tom	34877328	16 Jan 45
Tec 5	Carter, Edward H	42082644	16 Jan 45
Tec 5	Foamon, Elmer T	34855775	16 Jan 45
Tec 5	Foster, E Alonzo	33811061	16 Jan 45
Tec 5	Gisson, Luther	42037260	8 Sep 44
Tec 5	Martin, Charlie H	38629110	2 Feb 45
Tec 5	McCoy, Roosevelt	38629148	16 Jan 45

Tec 5	Moorman, Royal S	42082374	16 Jan 45
Tec 5	Perry, Roy	33806614	16 Jan 45
Tec 5	Senior, Julius	38601680	16 Jan 45
Tec 5	Upchurch, Floyd	34853471	16 Jan 45
Pfc	Birmingham, Lee	39128065	8 Sep 44
Pfc	Brandon, Willie J	34798087	16 Jan 45
Pfc	Brooks, Minor B	38184309	17 Aug 44
Pfc	Cain, Robert	34798559	16 Jan 45
Pfc	Davies, Eddie	38521281	16 Jan 45
Pfc	Dickerson, John J	37632680	16 Jan 45
Pfc	Fullmore, Levi	34853421 1/2	16 Jan 45
Pfc	Haigler, Cleve	34846193	16 Jan 45
Pfc	Hall, Jessie	38629114	16 Jan 45
Pfc	Hawkins, Edward	38491282	7 Feb 45
Pfc	Hill, Robert W	33752916	16 Jan 45
Pfc	Hollins, Carl W	37633109	16 Jan 45
Pfc	Huggins, Jr. Charles	34846023	2 Feb 45
Pfc	Key, Buran H	42103645	16 Jan 45
Pfc	Lewis, Thomas	37724330	2 Feb 45
Pfc	Lewis, Thomas	42082711	2 Feb 45
Pfc	Mills, Marvin S	39718212	16 Jan 45
Pfc	Mitchell, Floyd C	38547275	16 Jan 45
Pfc	Parker, James D	38600151	16 Jan 45
Pfc	Rader, Jr. Douglas	38599915	16 Jan 45
Pfc	Singleton, Izer	34849561	16 Jan 45
Pfc	Webb, Hollis	36946034	16 Jan 45
Pvt	Brown, Edward L	34846280	16 Jan 45
Pvt	Fisher, L. A.	38602103	16 Jan 45
Pvt	Holmes, Ernest	32997251	2 Feb 45
Pvt	Lett, Wilton	37633559	2 Feb 45
Pvt	Macklin, Clinton B	33854130	16 Jan 45
Pvt	Martin, Thomas	42017977	16 Jan 45
Pvt	Walker, Willie J	34877800	16 Jan 45
Pvt	Williams, Ollee	34071393	17 Aug 44

BY ORDER OF COLONEL SORLEY:

E. A. HURLOCK, JR
Capt., CE
Acting Adjutant

OFFICIAL:
E. A. HURLOCK, JR
Capt., CE
Acting Adjutant
<u>DISTRIBUTION "A"</u>
plus 1 ea EM conc

EXTRACT

The notation "plus 1 ea EM conc" under the distribution notice at the end of the document means that a copy was to be given to each enlisted man concerned. Since I am named in the orders I was given a copy.

"VOCO" means "verbal orders of commanding officer." The ranks, in the order listed, are staff sergeant, sergeant, technician fourth grade, corporal, technician fifth grade, private first class, private.

"ASN" means "army serial number." Every man in the army was assigned a serial number upon induction. All numbers consisted of eight digits. The second digit indicates in which of the nine army commands the soldier was inducted. For example, the second digit in my serial number (42066350) indicates that I was inducted in the second command, which, as I recall it, included New York, New Jersey and, I believe, Delaware.

There are some obvious typographical errors in these orders. I have copied the orders exactly as they were written, but I point out the following errata: S/Sgt James Elwood's serial number has one digit too many. Pfc. Levi Fullmore's number is obviously incorrect, since no serial number included fractions. The number quite probably is 34853421.

As the company clerk of Company F who maintained the service records of these men I am very certain, even after forty-nine years, that several of the men's names are misspelled in these orders. The corrected spellings should be S/Sgt Boynton, Jr. Willard; S/Sgt Nichols, Eddie W.; Tec 5 Foaman, Elmer T.; Tec 5 Glisson, Luther; Pvt. Fisher, L. E.

Finally, handwritten at the bottom of my copy, in a hand which I do not believe to be my own, are the following names: Jackson, R. V.; Cpl. Willie Williams; Sgt. Wright; Wilson, Boisy. I have no recollection as to how these names got written there. I do remember the men as members of Company F. My recollection is that Robert V. Jackson and Sgt. Richard Wright were New Yorkers. I believe Wright lived on 114th Street and that it was with him that I drank bad whiskey in Harlem on the night that we left to go back to Camp Claiborne after our furlough.

I suspect that the men whose names are listed at the bottom of the page may have had questions as to why their names did not appear in the orders to receive the awards and wanted me as company clerk to look into the matter. Or there could have been amended orders published, adding their names.

Chapter 3

Ossie Davis, in his stage play *Purlie Victorious,* which was presented at the Cort Theatre in New York in the 1960s, puts an interesting twist on the matter of combating segregation. In an intriguing scene where a white southerner is put "between a rock and a hard place" making advocacy for integration, Davis has Ol' Cap'n Cotchipee (Stonewall Jackson Cotchipee) speaking to Charlie (his twenty-five-year-old son), who has "integrationary ideas in his head," put there by Idella, one of the blacks on Ol' Cap'n's plantation. Charlie has had the temerity to express, in a local bar in Cotchipee County in south Georgia, the idea that integration was the law of the land, that it had to be obeyed and that everyone had to take a stand. For his pains Charlie was roughed up by the patrons of the bar and his actions were reported to his father by the sheriff. Ol' Cap'n Cotchipee brings Charlie and Idella to book. He tells Charlie that the sheriff had been there that morning, that he (Charlie) is a disgrace to the southland and that he (Cap'n Cotchipee) could kill Charlie with his own two hands if he (Charlie) weren't the last living drop of Cotchipee blood in Cotchipee County. Charlie's replies to all of these manifestations of Ol' Cap'n's exasperation are five responses of "Yessir." Ol' Cap'n responds to this with, "You trying to get non-violent with me, boy?"

Chapter 4

Dr. Hobart Jarrett, who taught at Langston University in Oklahoma at one time, tells me that he is sure that there are those who would argue that the black high school in Tulsa merits the ranking of flagship of the secondary school systems serving blacks in the Southwest, which ranking I assign to Dunbar High School of Little Rock. I recommend that those persons consult the book by Dr. Faustine Childress Jones, which I have cited in the Bibliography at the end of this book.

Chapter 6

As a family, we found the spending of an academic year in the environs of Paris to be a totally salutary experience for us all. Nona, at age five, when the conditions for second-language learning are optimal, was particularly advantaged by the experience. She mastered spoken French at a level which she probably would not have achieved had she had the experience at a later age. I believe, too, that the ease with which she moves around with people of different cultures had its genesis in the *Ecole maternelle de Courbevoie* and developed when she returned to the public schools in Spring Valley, West Nyack, and New City, New York. I believe, too, that this experience was not without some influence on her inviting an exchange student from Belgium to our home and on her going to Sweden on an exchange visit, both events occurring while she was in high school. I am sure that these experiences were good preparation for her for the social environment in which she found herself at Wellesley College, and perhaps even at Hofstra University Law School. I am certain that she is a better researcher at *Reader's Digest* for it all.

Charlene, too, undoubtedly is a better person for the experience. She learned to move about in a culture far removed from that of the southern United States in which she grew to adulthood. I will always remember her recounting of her experience in a stationery store trying, in French, to get the clerk to understand that she wanted to purchase a bottle of ink, and her description of the clerk's final exclamation, "Ohhhhhhhh. Ink!" I shall also always remember her relating her encounter with a rotating strike of bus drivers in Paris. Workers frequently rotated their stoppages from one bus line to the next without warning. The French army would then provide service in army trucks to fill in where the strikers left off. Charlene's French became serviceable enough for her to determine all of this. She would find out where to board a truck to take her to a stop where service was still intact, and from there she would take a bus to the *Gare St. Lazare* and then a train to Bécon-les-Bruyères. She continually reminds me that I have promised her a grand tour of all of these places.

The 1959–1960 academic year in France was without question the epitome of my experience as an advanced graduate student. Most of the career opportunities that have come my way are in some way related to the work that I accomplished during this period.

Chapter 8

In thinking about the rare instances in my public school career when I did not want to go to school because Africa and Africans were to be the subjects of our lessons on those days, I came late to realize that if my teachers had been black I would not have had these uncomfortable feelings. Even if they had come under the tutelage of John W.

Burgess himself at Columbia University, or of any of his disciples, they would have applied a revisionist spin to their presentations, as legions of black teachers did in the South. John W. Burgess, the dean of the Political Science Faculty at Columbia University in the 1890s, had documented, racist views about blacks and Africa. He, who was quoted during his heyday as having said, "A black skin means membership in a race of men which . . . has never created any civilization of any kind," trained a long line of white Africanists at Columbia.

My own justification for black studies programs is largely based on views expressed in 1971 by Sterling Stuckey, at the time chairman of the Afro-American Curriculum Committee at Northwestern University. First, I believe that such studies belong in the upper division of baccalaureate programs and not in associate degree programs. Stuckey convinced me of the injustice which white American scholars had perpetrated on African studies and of the "fabric of untruths" which numerous white experts on black Africa had elaborated to rationalize continued white control over African studies. From Stuckey's argument I also am convinced of the unacceptable role which the African Studies Association, a predominantly white scholarly organization of Africanists, played in all of this. (For an account of the struggle by black scholars within the African Studies Association to have some influence on the direction of the organization, see Rudy Johnson's *New York Times* article.)

Having been a victim of this vicious conspiracy, through teachers who, I am sure, learned whatever it is they knew about Africa from scholars with orientations inherited from the likes of Harvard's Louis Agassiz and Columbia's John Burgess, I was a ready convert to Stuckey's findings. (I never had a black teacher, from kindergarten through Ph.D.) Noting that African studies in 1971 were still dominated by all-white faculty, all-white students and "whitewashes" of much of the black experience, Stuckey made the point that it was these "newcomers" who were telling us that blacks in this country have only recently become interested in Africa, have no significant ties with Africa, and have contributed practically no scholarship on Africa. Further, Stuckey argued, these people now had the gall to want to inject ideological considerations into a field of study whose specialists heretofore had been above such practices. After these observations Stuckey then made a point which I had not considered beforehand but on which I joined him philosophically: African studies should become the heart of black studies.

Chapter 9

In 1983 when I retired from New York City Technical College I had intended to do some writing which I had postponed when I became an administrator in 1967. When I took another full-time administrative post at Bergen Community College within a week after retiring from NYC Tech, I again put aside the writing project. In 1991 I again began to think seriously about the events of the 1969 to 1971 era and my resolve to write a memoir centering on my career. I began searching my files for texts of speeches and for notes which I had made on various occasions with the objective of writing this memoir. I made efforts to contact men with whom I had served in the army to refresh my recollections of events related to World War II. I began to pull together and organize the writings I had done over the years since I began college teaching and to write this memoir.

In 1992 I began to notice that a genre of which I had not been aware was developing: memoirs of black academics. I notice that these academics are of my daughter's generation (Wellesley '76) and that the canon to which I hope this book belongs is short on contributors from the class of '49. But then, my friend and colleague Professor William E. Nelson of Ohio State University tells me that African-American biography is an area that is immensely underdeveloped. In any case, books by Stephen L. Carter, Henry Louis Gates, Jr., Gayle Pemberton, Brent Staples and Shelby Steele, which are cited in the Bibliography, are part of that canon I see emerging.

Chapter 10

In rereading my reflections in this chapter, some afterthoughts occur. When I think of the students who came to my office in late 1969 or in early 1970 to demand "an autonomous" black studies department and of my lukewarm attitude toward the activism that was ambient on the campus during the period, I recall the response which Martin Kilson gave students at Harvard who viewed him much the way that students viewed me. He told them that he was a scholar, not an activist. The position that I took was that when I could support their proposals I would do so with vigor and decisively. When I opposed their propositions, I would be silent. When I was silent, I told them, any pressure would bring comments that would not be helpful to their cause. In thinking on all of this now, I am reminded that I and others at New York City Community College took a different view of the atmosphere that prevailed on that campus than that which was suggested in the *New York Times* article of 1 June 1969 ("College with Many Nonwhites"). I also now wonder if the facts which are provided in M. A. Farber's *New York Times* article were a harbinger of, or in a *post hoc ergo propter hoc* relationship with, the atmosphere which I perceived later on that campus. I look forward to some day reading a thorough, objective study of black studies programs in lower-division colleges. (New York City Technical College is no longer a lower-division college, so the question is moot as it pertains to that institution.)

In the aftermath of writing this memoir I have synthesized my sense of who I am by attributing a heretofore unprecedented role to my Jamaican-American heritage. The interesting thing about all of this is that this synthesis resulted from ideas or suggestions which came to me from two persons, neither of whom is of Jamaican-American heritage, but with each of whom I have a common bond: membership in Alpha Phi Alpha Fraternity, Inc. These Brothers-in-Alpha are William E. Nelson, Jr., and Paul Robeson, Jr. These two men have no idea at all of the influence that they or their ideas have had on me in this instance. While Nelson has read the manuscript, commented on it, disagreed with me on some of my more conservative positions on issues such as black studies and the black power movement, his careful reading of it suggested to him that I should address "the impact of Jamaican culture" on the professional mobility of myself and on that of my siblings. Paul Robeson, Jr., on the other hand, knows me better than does William Nelson, Jr., but has not read my manuscript. His influence on my thinking has come solely through my reading of his *Paul Robeson, Jr. Speaks to America*.

I have concluded that my arrogant position that I am as good as anyone else, that I can do anything that anyone else with the level of intelligence that I have can do, is unaffected by the naysayers around me and that if I can but get the opportunity to try I can achieve whatever anyone else with the same level of intelligence can achieve, no matter what his race or ethnic background. What differences, if any, exist in intelligence between the races I do not know. What I do know is that I have taught black students who are as bright as any white students that I have taught. Some of my black students were brighter than I am and than were some of the white students whom I have taught. What William Nelson has suggested to me is that I look at the hypothesis that my Jamaican-American heritage has something to do with my achievement and that of my brother and sisters. Paul Robeson's proposition that America is a mosaic of cultures with each ethnic group deserving equal status suggests to me that my Jamaican-American heritage may have as much to contribute to the explanation of my achievement as anything else. Maybe, as Nelson suggests, and as Robeson's proposition hypothesizes, my culture comes closer to explaining what I have become than does my race.

Chapter 11

While I am proud of the recognition which I received as a student and which is manifest in my certificate from the *Ecole de préparation et de perfectionnement des professeurs de français à l'étranger* at the Sorbonne and as a college teacher as is manifest in the Outstanding Teacher Award given me by the Alumni Association of New York City Community College, my greatest regret as pertains to my career is that I did not make a mark as a productive scholar during the thirty-four years that I served on faculties of four colleges in four states.

Chapter 12

My experience at Bergen Community College served as a most fitting close to my career as a college administrator. I was able to discharge most of the responsibilities assigned to me at Bergen from the apperceptive background I had developed at New York City Technical College. This enabled me to focus on the first-time-ever responsibility I had as affirmative action officer. Ironically, even in this instance my experience came into play; as affirmative action officer I was ever mindful of the experience I had had in Little Rock, where I was told that my application for a position could not be considered because they had "nothing to go on for colored." As the affirmative action officer at Bergen Community College I made sure that the policy which was already in place had teeth. Everyone who had authority to make appointments for any position in the college, from building cleaners to deanships, was carefully briefed by me and had "something to go on" which was inclusive. I monitored the candidate pools and the recommendations for appointments. I read the candidate evaluations. I held people accountable. Two of the appointments which were made at that institution as a result of my intervention as affirmative action officer are among the most satisfying personal achievements of my thirty-four-year career in higher education. I do not apologize for affirmative action as a policy. I wish affirmative action had been a national policy in 1950!

Chapter 13

I always considered it a personal responsibility to help advance the interests of black people in my community and, as an educator, to lend my effort to improving the achievement of black students particularly. Thus, I was one of the founding members of the Rockland Negro Scholarship Fund, which has an exemplary record in raising and awarding scholarship funds in the amount of more than $410,000 since its inception in 1965. I worked for many years as chairman of the education committee of the Nyack branch of the NAACP to help to improve the learning environment for black students in all of the schools in Rockland County. As a founding member of Eta Chi Lambda chapter of Alpha Phi Alpha Fraternity, Inc., in Rockland County, I was instrumental in committing it to the fraternity's national program motto: "Go to High School, Go to College." I am proud of our record of identifying black male high school students, encouraging them to consider attending college and helping them to do so.

I venture to say that those of us who organized Eta Chi Lambda chapter of Alpha Phi Alpha Fraternity, Inc., constituted a substantial percentage of the college-trained black men resident in Rockland County in 1960! Further, I believe that this group was a catalyst which precipitated the increase in the number of black males considering college attendance as an option, particularly in the years before the founding of Rockland Community College.

As an agent for change in schools in Rockland, I had my most disappointing experience with the Clarkstown School District, where I live and where my daughter attended school from the second grade through the twelfth grade. In my opinion, from the perspective of educational quality and effectiveness, this school district was and is first-rate. I believe that the education which Nona received in this district is validated by the fact that she was admitted to one of the highly selective (and expensive) women's colleges in this country and, in addition, was prepared to succeed academically there, which she did. It is in the area of intercultural understanding that I think this school district left something to be desired.

At the time when Dr. Martin Luther King, Jr., was assassinated, I noted what I sensed as a sort of misunderstanding of the significance of, or a distancing of itself from, this tragic event by the totally white school board and administration. Other districts in the county reacted officially in ways that organizations do when persons of significance to their patrons meet with tragedy. Clarkstown did not. From that time I have observed what I have read as something less than an empathetic feeling on the part of the Clarkstown school administration toward blacks. The instance when I went to confer with the superintendent of schools over the matter of the complaint of my neighbor about the "Mammy Pleasant" presentation at Clarkstown High School North is another example. In making my advocacy for my neighbor's complaint I had some mixed feelings as an academic, given the question of academic freedom involved. I rationalized my action by reminding myself that the primary issue then was the attitude of the school administration in the face of a complaint from a black patron. As I said at the time, my concern was more that the superintendent could not understand how anyone could be offended by the portrayal of "Mammy Pleasant" than it was that he could not or would not apologize to her for any offense which she might have experienced from it.

Now, more than twenty years later, the issue has resurfaced at Clarkstown High School. This time I was not involved and know only what I have read in the *Rockland Journal-News*. The end result in this instance was totally different from that following the one in which I was involved. Nevertheless, I am reluctant to feel that *we* won on this one. If we won, our victory was pyrrhic because freedom of speech lost ground. I am between the same rock and hard place that I was on the "Mammy Pleasant" incident. From the newspaper article which appeared on November 4, 1994, we are able to get the following picture.

Shortly before the first issue of the Clarkstown High School North newspaper for the 1994–1995 school year went to press, Chris Golde, the faculty adviser, was told that his appointment as adviser to the *Ram's Horn* would not be extended after his having previously been reappointed for fifteen consecutive years. It appears that the September 1993 issue of the student newspaper had carried "a controversial article" on the editorial page arguing against affirmative action and contending that blacks, Hispanics and other racial minorities are academically inferior to whites. Three members of the school board are reported to have said that this article is just "the straw that broke the camel's back." We are led to presume that a failing of Mr. Golde's was his failure to teach students about the ramifications associated with being controversial.

My own reaction to all of this? I am encouraged by the statement attributed to Mrs. Gail Koss, a member of the school board. She was quoted as saying, "The article just countered everything we are trying to teach in the system." Further, she is reported to have said that minority students had been hurt. I am reassured by Mrs. Koss' coming forth on the issue of the feelings of minority people. I cannot recall any previous instance in which a member of the school board in Clarkstown ever made a statement showing an understanding of, much less an empathy for, minority people. Maybe a new ambiance is extant in this school district. Mr. Pantano has been retired from the board by the voters too.

Bibliography

Many books, magazine and newspaper articles, syndicated columns, essays, and the like, contributed to the thinking which I brought to events and issues which I confronted during the tumultuous late 1960s and early 1970s. Ultimately, ideas gleaned from these sources have surely found their way into this book. In the effort to retrace the paths to my positions on issues, persons and events during the late 1960s and early 1970s, I looked through my personal library collection and created a selected bibliography of the books which I read during the period from 1963 to 1971. Fortunately, they were available to be cited here. In addition, I searched my newspaper clipping file (begun in 1963, and now consisting of several thousand clippings) and culled forty-two from the period 1963–1971 which deal with issues, persons and events which engaged me and which I engaged during that period. There are, of course, magazine and journal articles which I consulted in the library at New York

City Community College and elsewhere. These, too, obviously contributed to my thinking, but cannot be cited, since I do not remember them. Alas, at age forty-eight I did not have the foresight to plan for the day at age sixty-nine when I would be trying to track my sources in the effort to document the development of my views.

Also included in this Bibliography are books, articles and letters which postdate those which formed my thinking in the tumultuous 1960s and 1970s. Ideas in these works also contributed to the mind-set of a brother like me and require my acknowledgment.

Books

Breitman, George, ed., *Malcolm X Speaks* (New York: Grove Press, 1965).

Carmichael, Stokely, & Charles V. Hamilton, *Black Power* (New York: Vintage Books, 1967).

Carter, Stephen L., *Reflections of an Affirmative Action Baby* (New York: Basic Books, 1991).

Caute, David, *Frantz Fanon* (New York: Viking Press, 1970).

Cruse, Harold, *The Crisis of the Negro Intellectual* (New York: Morrow, 1967).

Davis, Ossie, *Purlie Victorious: A Comedy in Three Acts* (New York: Samuel French, 1961).

Fanon, Frantz, *Toward the African Revolution: Political Essays* (New York: Grove Press, 1967).

———, *Black Skin, White Masks* (New York: Grove Press, 1968).

Frazier, E. Franklin, *The Negro in the United States* (rev. ed.) (New York: Macmillan, 1958).

———, *Black Bourgeoisie* (New York: Free Press, 1965).

Gates, Henry Louis, Jr., *Colored People: A Memoir* (New York: Alfred A. Knopf, 1994).

Geismar, Peter, *Fanon* (New York: Dial Press, 1971).

Gendzier, Irene L., *Frantz Fanon: A Critical Study* (New York: Pantheon, 1973).

Gregory, Dick, *Nigger* (New York: Pocket Books, 1964).

———, *The Shadow That Scares Me* (New York: Pocket Books, 1968).

———, *Write Me In!* (New York: Bantam Books, 1968).

Grier, William H., & Price M. Cobbs, *Black Rage* (New York: Bantam Books, 1968).

Hall, Bruce Edward, *Diamond Street* (New York: Black Dome Press, 1994).

Jones, Faustine Childress, *A Traditional Model of Educational Excellence: Dunbar High School of Little Rock, Arkansas* (Washington, D.C.: Howard University Press, 1981).

King, Martin Luther, Jr., *Strength to Love* (New York: Pocket Books, 1964).

———, *Stride Toward Freedom: The Montgomery Story* (New York: Ballantine Books, 1960).

———, *Where Do We Go from Here: Chaos or Community?* (New York: Bantam Books, 1968).

Lincoln, C. Eric, *The Black Muslims in America* (Boston: Beacon Press, 1961).

Miller, William Robert, *Martin Luther King, Jr.: His Life, Martyrdom and Meaning for the World* (New York: Avon Books, 1969).

Pemberton, Gayle, *The Hottest Water in Chicago: On Family, Race, Time and American Culture* (Boston: Faber and Faber, 1992).

Robeson, Paul, Jr., *Paul Robeson, Jr. Speaks to America* (New Brunswick, N.J.: Rutgers University Press, 1993).

Rudwick, Elliott M., *W.E.B. DuBois: Propagandist of the Negro Protest* (New York: Atheneum, 1969).

Silberman, Charles E., *Crisis in Black and White* (New York: Vintage Books, 1964).

Staples, Brent, *Parallel Time: Growing Up in Black and White* (New York: Pantheon Books, 1994).

Steele, Shelby, *The Content of Our Character: A New Vision of Race in America* (New York: St. Martin's Press, 1990).

Washington, Booker T., *Up from Slavery* (New York: Bantam Books, 1963).

Williams, John A., *This Is My Country Too* (New York: Signet Books, 1966).

X, Malcolm, *The Autobiography of Malcolm X: With the Assistance of Alex Haley* (New York: Grove Press, 1965).

Young, Whitney M., Jr., *Beyond Racism* (New York: McGraw-Hill, 1969).

Articles and Letters

The news articles cited here are from my collection and are either background material for some of my thinking (in regard to the Black Panthers, Rap Brown, open enrollment, etc.) or press reaction to some of the events in which I was involved or about which I expressed opinions publicly (e.g., school board elections in Nyack).

"Africa Surprises Black Americans," *New York Times*, 6 Sep. 1970.

Akar, John J., "Is Black Beautiful to Africans?" *New York Times*, 31 Oct. 1970.

"Alumni of C.C.N.Y. Press for Change," *New York Times*, 12 Apr. 1970.

"C.C.N.Y. Will Add to Ethnic Studies," *New York Times*, 4 Apr. 1971.

"Campaign Tactics Hit, Anonymity Flailed," *Record*, 11 May 1970.

"Carmichael Questioned Secretly by Senate Security Committee," *New York Times*, 26 Mar. 1970.

"A College Course in Chaos," *Rockland Journal-News*, 15 Sep. 1970.

"College with Many Nonwhites Avoids the Turmoil," *New York Times*, 1 Jun. 1969.

Conkling, F. Wheeler, letter, "Poor Campaign Tactics," *Rockland Journal-News*, 13 May 1970.

Corcoran, David, "TaxPayers Stunned: It's Yes on Nyack Budget," *Record*, 7 May 1970.

"Defenders of Campus Freedom," *New York Times*, 22 Nov. 1970.

Delaney, Paul, "Panther Parley Failure," *New York Times*, 30 Nov. 1970.

"ESD Hires 1st Negroes for 'White Collar' Jobs," *Arkansas Gazette*, 2 Mar. 1962.

Faber, Harold, "Hudson Casts New Light on Its Red-Light Past," *New York Times*, 21 Oct. 1994.

Farber, M. A., "Minority Groups on Rise in City U.," *New York Times*, 15 Dec. 1967.

Franklin, Ben A., "Rap Brown Is the Man Who Wasn't There," *New York Times*, 10 May 1970.

Giniger, Henry, "A Famous Paris College Closed after Take-Over by New Left," *New York Times,* 5 Apr. 1971.

Handler, M. S., "N.A.A.C.P. Is Told It Faces a Choice," *New York Times,* 30 Jun. 1965.

Hechinger, Fred M., "To Live or Not to Live with Campus Coercion," *New York Times,* 6 Apr. 1970.

Herbers, John, "Tour of 7 Cities Indicates Mood of Negro Is Uneasy," *New York Times,* 1 Jun. 1969.

Hook, Sidney, "Campus Terror: An Indictment," *New York Times,* 22 Oct. 1970.

Hunter, Charlayne, "Confusion Feared in Black Studies," *New York Times,* 8 Mar. 1970.

Johnson, Rudy, "Parley Stresses African Heritage," *New York Times,* 10 May 1970.

Johnson, Thomas A., "African Studies Center at Cornell Develops Practical and Scholarly Skills," *New York Times,* 5 Jan. 1971.

Kilson, Martin, letter, "Ethnocentric Insider-Outsider Doctrine," *New York Times,* 21 Dec. 1972.

Kirk, Grayson, "Limits of Academic Tolerance," *New York Times,* 2 Jan. 1971.

Kourtakis, Kim, "Teacher Loses Adviser Job Due to Story," *Rockland Journal-News,* 4 Nov. 1994, p. B7.

Leibenstein, Harvey, letter, "Faculty Deliberations," *New York Times,* 29 Jun. 1969.

Lomax, Louis, letter, "Revolution—1969," *New York Times,* 19 Jul. 1969.

McKissick, Floyd, "From a Black Point of View: Black Dilemma—Black Power," *New York Amsterdam News,* 25 Oct. 1969.

Morsell, John A., letter, "Futility of Black Self-Segregation," *New York Times*, 7 Mar. 1968.

Ng'weno, Hilary, "The Panthers: An African's View," *New York Times*, 2 Oct. 1970.

" 'Non-Violent' Out of S.N.C.C's Name," *New York Times*, 23 Jul. 1969.

Nordheimer, Jon, "Black 'Nation' Vexes Mississippi," *New York Times*, 10 Apr. 1971.

"Panelists Assail View on Black I.Q.," *New York Times*, 23 Nov. 1969.

Raspberry, William, "Black Identity May Come First," *Record*, 23 Sep. 1970.

Reinhold, Robert, "Liberal Scholar Uneasy on Youth," *New York Times*, 7 Jul. 1969.

"The Schools Win," *Record*, 13 May 1970.

Schumach, Murray, "Faculty at City U. Fears Erosion of Standards and of Its Authority," *New York Times*, 14 Dec. 1969.

Stuckey, Sterling, "Black Studies and White Myths," *New York Times*, 13 Feb. 1971.

Taylor, Harold, "We Need Radicals," *New York Times*, 27 Feb. 1971.

"Threat to Campus Freedom," *New York Times*, 27 Apr. 1971.

Wheeldin, Don, "Uncle Tom Is Libeled by Blacks," *Record*, 17 Dec. 1969.

Index

Note: HD = Harry Dunbar.

academic freedom, racial stereotypes vs., 93–94
A.M.E. Zion Church *see* African Methodist Episcopal Zion Church
Africa, school lessons on, 13, 212–214
African Methodist Episcopal Zion Church, 1, 3, 4, 12, 60
African status, affected, 116–117
African Studies Association, 213
Agassiz, Louis, 213
Agnew, Spiro T., 102–105, 125–126
Alpha Kappa Alpha Sorority, 112
Alpha Phi Alpha Fraternity, Inc., 52, 53, 63, 65, 81, 109–113, 216
   Alpha Gamma Lambda chapter, 109

Eta chapter, 62, 111
Eta Chi Lambda chapter, 111–113, 119–120, 219–220
   establishment of, 110–111
   HD's positions in, 112, 119
Pi Lambda chapter, 62–64
positions of HD in, 113
American Airlines, 155–161
   apology to HD from, 160
   discourtesy of, toward non-whites, 155–156, 160–161
   HD's letter to, 156–159
American Church (France), 86–87
American Federation of Teachers, 196
American Jewish Congress, 94
Angiello, Roanne, 190–191
Antioch College, 119
Appalachian State College, 92
Arkansas AM&N College, 58, 61

Arkansas Baptist College, 58–60
Arkansas Democrat, 62, 64
Arkansas Gazette, 67–68
Army University Center (AUC), 26, 42–44, 45
   HD as student at, 43–44
   integration at, 26, 43

Balakian, Anna, 72
Baron, E., 67–68
Barone, Anthony, 19
Bassin, Milton, 130–131
Bates, Daisy, 78
Baudin, Maurice, 50, 72
BCC *see* Bergen Community College
Beasley, Charles, 56
Bécon-les-Bruyères, 82–83, 86
Bédé, Jean Albert, 73, 74
Bellessort, André, 84
Bergen Community College (BCC), 84, 122, 175–191, 193
   administrative organization at, 186–191
   affirmative action at, 178–179, 218–219
   ethnic diversity of faculty, 176–177
   HD's positions at:
      affirmative action officer, 178, 184, 218–219
      assistant dean of instruction, 175–176
      associate dean, 177
      dean of Evening Division, 176
      dean of the faculty, 177
      Office of Academic Affairs, 190–191
      tenured professor, 177
   labor-relations culture at, 179–186, 189
   vs. New York City Technical College, 177–183, 187–188
Berlin, Isaiah, 46
Best, Katherine, 14
"The Best of Times, the Worst of Times," 96–108
Bibliothèque nationale (France), 80, 83
"black":
   HD's concept of self as, 113–116
   as term of racial identity, 4
black college mission statement (HD), 57
Black History Month, 196
"Black Personality Disorders: The Legacy of White Racism," 91
black power, 95, 100, 131–142
   danger of, 138–139
   definitions of, 133–134
   as divisive force, 136–138
   vs. nonviolence, 140
   philosophy of, 134–135
   as racism, 136, 138
   Wright's defense of, 140–142
   See also violence by blacks
"Black Power: Pernicious Doctrine and Cruel Hoax," 132–140
black students:
   deterioration of schools and, 151
   dropouts among, 91
   HD as ombudsman for parents of, 92–94
   positive effect of faculty on, 57
   tutoring center for, 117–119

black studies programs, 213–214, 215–216
  HD's position on, 147, 150–151
  proposal for, at NYCCC, 129–130
blacks:
  advances of, positive action and, 97–98, 100
  importance of civic participation by, 107–108
  memoirs of, 215
  textbook treatment of, 13, 194–197
Blount, Walter, 110–111, 193
Booker, John Robert, 62, 63
Boy Scouts, HD in, 19–20
Branch, Clarence, 110, 111
Brewer, Walter, 143
Brickman, William, 74, 79–80, 90
Briggs, Ernest, 58, 59, 65–66
Brightbill, Mary, 5–6
Brinkman, Albert, 121–122
Brisbane, Era, 76
Bronx Community College, CUNY, 98
Brooke, Edward, 98, 105
Brooklyn College, CUNY, 117, 128, 172
Brown, Rap, 98, 104
Brown, Roscoe, 51
Brée, Germaine, 50, 72–74, 80
Burgess, John W., 13, 212–214

Campbell, Ann, 50
Camus, Albert, 74–75
Carmichael, Stokely, 98, 104, 133–135, 141
Castro, Fidel, 188
CCNY (City College of New York), CUNY, 11, 82
Central High School, court-ordered desegregation of, 78
Channing, William Henry, 199–200
Christian Association, HD as member of, 51
City College of New York (CCNY), CUNY, 11, 82
City University of New York (CUNY):
  Academic Affairs Office, 169
  Graduate Center, 172
  open admissions at, 123–126
  University Faculty Development Program, HD as coordinator of, 171–173
  See also individual college names
Civil Rights Act, 151
Civil War, 117
Claflin College, 58
Clark College, 56
Clarke, John Henrik, 47
Clarkstown School District, 194–197
  intercultural relations and, 220–222
  "Mammy Pleasant" incident in, 93–94, 221
Clinkscale, Arlene, 122
Cobb, Jewell Plummer, 50
Cohen, Oscar, 122
Colston, James, 51
Columbia University, 73, 74, 111, 212–214
Computers:
  faculty retraining in, HD as coordinator of, 169–170
  HD's use of, 167–169, 171
Concord magazine, 84
Congress of Racial Equality (CORE), 133, 136

Cooke, Leonard, 114, 122
CORE (Congress of Racial Equality), 133, 136
Cornell University, 112
Cousin, Victor, 143
Crandall, Robert L., 156
Crawford, Roy, 58–59
Cunningham, Arthur, 110
CUNY *see* City University of New York

Davis, Milton, 113
Davis, Ossie, 209–210
Delta Sigma Theta Sorority, 112
Dickens, Charles, 96–97
Dissertation (HD), 114, 143
  research on, in France, 80, 83–85
  research design for, 78–80
  topic of, 73–74
Donaghey College, 68
Donelson, Alfrado, 112
Donelson, Ulysses, 112
Dorsey, Rufus, 56, 57
Dunbar, Catherine (HD's sister), 2, 9–10, 33, 202–205
Dunbar, Cora Charlene (née Whitlow; HD's wife), 78, 80, 86, 153
  Little Rock background of, 69–70
  year in France and, 211–212
Dunbar, Elma Alexandria (née Russell-Brown; HD's mother), 7–11, 17–18, 153, 202–203
  influence of, on HD, 6, 8–9
Dunbar, Harry B.:
  birth of, 1
  childhood and adolescence of, 12–23
  elementary education of, 12–14
    Preliminary Certificate, 18
  first jobs of, 21–23
  inducted into army, 25
  marriage of, 69
  secondary education of, 5–6, 18–20
    diploma, 8
  See also specific topics and institutions
Dunbar, Henry (HD's brother), 9, 11–12
Dunbar, Ida (HD's sister), 2, 9, 11, 202, 204
Dunbar, Louise (HD's sister), 2, 9–11, 70, 202, 204
Dunbar, Nona (HD's daughter), 80, 83, 93, 220
  year in France and, 85–86, 211
Dunbar, Shafter Nathan (HD's father), 1–7, 9–10, 17, 18, 205
  influence of, on HD, 5–6, 9
  as minister, 4, 12, 18
  as street preacher in Harlem, 3–4
Dunbar High School, 59–61
Dunbar Junior College *see* Paul Laurence Dunbar Junior College
Durand, Louis, 84–85

Ecole normale supérieure, 73–74, 78–80, 85, 143
Elam, Harryette, 62
England, HD in, during World War II, 35–37, 163
L'Etranger (*The Stranger*), 74–75

Faber, Harold, 201–203
faculty union(s), 179–186
   vs. BCC administration,
     183–185, 189
   at BCC and NYC Tech,
     179–183
     collective bargaining and,
       179–180, 182–184, 186
     inception of, 183
     leadership of, 180–182
     deference of BCC faculty to,
       185–186
Farber, M. A., 216
Farrington, Leona, 118
Federal Aviation Administration, 160
"Fidus" papers, 83–84, 114, 166
First Baptist Church, 95, 96
Fisk University, 110, 141
Flacelière, Robert, 85
Florida A&M College, 111
France, 187, 211–212
   absence of racism in, 87
   HD in:
     for dissertation research,
       81–87, 212
     for Sorbonne seminar,
       76–77, 218
     during World War II,
       37–41
La France au Vingtième Siècle
   (*France in the Twentieth Century*), 72–73
Francis Scott Key Junior High School 117, HD as teacher at, 71–72, 76, 78
Frazier, Constance, 122
Frazier, E. Franklin, 117
French Review, 83
Fulbright Award, granted to HD, 76–77

Garvey, Marcus, 1, 4
Gertz department store, HD employed at, 70
G.I. Bill of Rights, 45
Gilkey, William, 63
Glasser, Israel, 130
"Go to High School, Go to College," 112, 219
Goff, William, 14
Golde, Chris, 221–222
Goldstein, Leon, 188
Goode, Mal, 112
Gordon, Mae, 15
Gregory, Dick, 107
Guam, HD in, during World War II, 42–43
gun control laws, 99–100, 107

Halliburton, Warren, 58, 59
Hanscom, James, 74
Hare, Baynard, 36, 38, 41, 42
Harris, M. Lafayette, 63
Harvard Medical School, 62
Harvard University, 132, 213, 215
Harvey, Edward, 83
Hegwood, Vivian, 61
Henry, Charles D., 66
history, rewriting of, 194–197
Hitler, Adolf, 101
Hofstra University, 11, 211
Holland, Albert, 52, 111
Holland, Laurence, 111
Howard University, 12, 60, 133
Hudgins, William R., 115
Hudson, New York, 15–18, 201–205
Hughes, Langston, 149–150
Hunter College, CUNY, 10, 172

Ish, G. W. S., 62

Jackson, Uriel, 59
Jamaica, 152–155, 168
  as black-run country, 153–154
  class discrimination in,
    154–155
  HD's parents and, 1–2, 7–8,
    10, 12, 152
Jamaican-American heritage,
  role of, in HD's life,
  216–217
Jarrett, Hobart, 210
Jarvis Christian College, 76
Jet magazine, 62
John Hay Whitney Foundation,
  80, 168
  fellowship awarded to HD, 80
Jones, Faustine Childress, 60, 211
Jones, Robert W., 111
Jones High School, 60–61

Kenyon College, 83
Kilson, Martin, 215
King, Martin Luther, Jr., 99,
  136–137, 220
Kingsborough Community College, CUNY, 188
Knoxville College, 98
Koss, Gail, 222
Kugler, Israel, 180

Lacour-Gayet, Robert, 72–73,
  75–76
Langston University, 58, 210
Lanson, Gustave, 77
LeClerc, Paul, 172
Lehman College, CUNY,
  172–173
Little Rock, Arkansas, 59–60,
  64–68, 69–70
  college closings in, 67–68

  court-ordered desegregation
    in, 78
  HD in, 59–66
  school board of, 67
  U.S. Employment Service in,
    64–65, 97
  Little Rock Junior College,
    67–68
London School of Economics,
  86
Lopez-Isa, Jose, 184–185, 188–191
Louisville Municipal College, 56

Mabry, Ralph and Gwendolyn,
  81–82
MacCalman, Kenneth R.,
  118–120
Maddox, Lester G., 103
Marcus Aurelius, 101
McCants, Coolidge, 51, 52, 81
McGirt, Paul, 76–77
McKissick, Floyd, 133–135
Meharry Medical College, 62
melting-pot ideology, 152–153,
  161–162
Mencken, H. L., 40, 186
Middle States Association of
  Schools and Colleges,
  HD as evaluator for, 92,
  146
Middletown High School, 18, 31
Miles College, 141
Morgan State College, 110
Morris, Mamie, 56
Mynatt, Maurice, 65

NAACP *see* National Association for the Advancement of Colored People
Nanuet Jewish Center, 90–91

Nanuet Junior-Senior High
    School, 89–92
Nathaniel Hawthorne Junior
    High School, HD as
    teacher at, 43–44
National Association for the
    Advancement of Colored
    People (NAACP), 51, 151
  Crisis, 106
  Nyack branch of, 92–94,
    117–122
  HD as chairman of education committee, 92, 95,
    114, 117, 219
National Conference on Black
    Power, 95
National Rifle Association, 107
Nelson, William E., 215, 216–217
Nesbitt, Zephaniah, 132
New York City:
  Bedford-Stuyvesant, 130
  Board of Education, 70–71
  Department of Parks, HD
    employed by, 70
  Harlem, 3, 33
  licensure process for teachers
    in, 71
  Public Library, 80
New York City Community
    College (NYCCC),
    CUNY, 84, 125, 149–150
  admission to, 128
  Alumni Association of, 199,
    218
  "Black Power" panel at,
    131–132
    See also black power
  black studies and, 147, 150–151,
    216
  black studies proposal for,
    129–130
  disciplinary hearing at,
    144–146
  early history of, 127–128
  Faculty Council, 129–130
  HD as chairman of curriculum committee, 126, 129
  foreign-language program,
    142–143
  HD as coordinator of, 128,
    131
  formerly New York State
    Institute of Arts and Sciences, 127
  HD's positions at, 120
    assistant professor, 127
    associate professor, 129
    dean of Division of Liberal
      Arts and Sciences, 129
    professor, 129
  open admissions at, 125,
    128–129
  and Police Bomb Squad, 147
  recruitment for, 143–144
  redesignated as New York
    City Technical College,
    166–167
    See also New York City Technical College
New York City Employees
    Retirement System, 167
New York City Teachers Retirement System, 167, 171
New York City Technical College, 168, 175, 216
  vs. Bergen Community College, 177–183, 187–188
  formerly New York City
    Community College,
    166
  HD as associate dean at, 187
  HD's terminal leave from, 174

labor-relations culture at, 179–183
student population at, 177–178
See also New York City Community College
New York State Education Department, 153
New York State Institute of Arts and Sciences, 127
New York Times, 15, 85, 89, 175, 201, 216
New York University (NYU), 12, 81, 110, 143
  the Commons, 52–53
  faculty at, 50–51, 72–73
  HD in doctoral program at, 72
  See also dissertation
  HD as graduate student at, 58, 75–76, 78
  HD as undergraduate at, 45, 49–53
  intellectual life at, 49–50
  placement service, 53
  School of Education, 72, 75
New York World Telegram and Sun, 71
Nixon, Richard, 62, 102–103, 105
Nonviolence, importance of, 102, 140
Nordstrom, Carl, 117, 118
North Carolina College, 77
North Central Association of Colleges and Schools, 59
Northwestern University, 213
Nyack School District, 92, 104
  instructional groupings of pupils in, 120–122
  tutoring center for blacks in, 117–119
NYCCC *see* New York City Community College

NYU *see* New York University

Ohio State University, 215
Olinger, Henri, 50, 72
"On Being a Negro in America circa 1966," 91
open admissions:
  at CUNY, 123–126
  at NYCCC, 125, 128–129
Ozell, Sutton, 113

Pantano, Joseph, 194–197, 222
Paul Laurence Dunbar Junior College, 60–63, 66–68, 69
  closing of, 67–68
  HD as instructor at, 58, 60, 66
  debating team coach, 61–62
  dramatic coach, 61
Pearman, Reginald, 51, 52
Le Petit Prince (*The Little Prince*), 75
Philander Smith College, 58, 60, 63, 65–66, 69
Pierce, Samuel, 112
Pomerance, Cybèle, 72
Potgieter, James and Joyce, 86
Powell, Adam Clayton, 51, 133
Prairie View A&M College, 58
Princeton University, 98
Proctor, Samuel, 98
public speaking (HD), 90–92, 94–95
  "The Best of Times, the Worst of Times," 96–108
  "Black Personality Disorders: The Legacy of White Racism," 91

"On Being a Negro in America circa 1966," 91
panel discussion on black power, 131–140
publications (HD), 83–84
Purlie Victorious, 47, 209–210

Queens College, CUNY, 11

"Race Related Problems," 140–142
racial stereotypes, academic freedom vs., 93–94
Reader's Digest, 211
Reed College, 86
Reid, Alban, 188
research pursuits (HD):
  extracting meaning from texts, 74–76
  identifying author of Fidus papers, 83–84, 114, 166
  See also dissertation
retirement (HD):
  decision on, 171, 173
  planning for, 167
    fellowship leave and, 167–171
  postponed, 175–176
  terminal leave prior to, 174
Revue des deux mondes, 83
Robert Gair Company, 22
Robeson, Paul, Jr., 161, 216–217
Rockefeller, Nelson, 130
Rockefeller, Winthrop, 66
Rockland Community College, 10, 220
  Advisory Board of, HD as vice-chairman of, 168

Rockland County Foreign Language Teachers Association, HD as chairman of, 91
Rockland Journal-News, 123–124, 194, 221
Rockland Negro Scholarship Fund, 219
Rockland Psychiatric Center, HD on Board of Visitors of, 193
Rothlein, Mary, 166, 169, 172, 174
Russell-Brown, Isabel (HD's aunt), 8
Rust College, HD as instructor at, 53, 55–57
  effect of faculty on students at, 57
Rutgers University, 119

Saint-Exupéry, Antoine de, 75
Schlesinger, Arthur, 162
Schwerin, Ursula, 167, 174
Shanker, Albert, 196–197
Shaw, Thomas, 188
Shorter College, 60
Shropshire, Jackie L., 62–63
Sigma Gamma Rho Sorority, 61
Singer, Lester, 130, 132, 150, 188
Sisco, Russell, 110
Skinner, Elliott, 51
Smith, Robert J., 143
SNCC (Student Nonviolent Coordinating Committee), 133, 135
Sorbonne (France), 76–77, 218
  Mention Très Honorable, HD awarded, 77
Southern Association of Schools and Colleges, 56

State University of New York, 84
 Community College Faculty Senate, HD as delegate to, 129
 Education Opportunity Center, confrontation over, 130–131
 Faculty Research Foundation, grant to HD from, 84, 166–167
Stuckey, Sterling, 13, 213–214
Student Nonviolent Coordinating Committee (SNCC), 133, 135
Sussman, Herbert, 146
Sutton, Ozell, 62, 63

"T-Town," 65–66
A Tale of Two Cities, 96
Talladega College, 62
Tappan Zee High School, 5–6, 8, 10
Tennessee A&I State College, 63, 92, 110, 111, 141
tenure, 186
Texas Southern College, 59
textual analysis (teaching method), 75–76
1325th Engineer General Service Regiment, 25–42, 46, 114
 and Battle of the Bulge, 38
 at Camp Claiborne, 25–34
 at Camp Shanks, 35
 destruction of army records on, 39–40
 in England, 35–37
 in France, 37–41
 General Orders No. 3, 205–209
 in Guam, 42–43
 HD as company clerk, 31, 34, 42, 209
 officer corps of, 28, 30–31
 punishment in, 29
 and Rhineland Campaign Medal, 39
 riot involving, 34
 trainers for, 29–31
 training of, 31–33
Thurmond, Strom, 104–105, 107
time management, 170–171
Togo (African Republic), 99

unions *see* faculty union(s)
Unitarian Fellowship of Rockland County, 117–120
United Electrical Radio and Machine Workers of America (UERMWA), 10, 22–23
United Methodist Church, 60
U.S. Army:
 assessment of, 162–163
 vs. civilian life, 45–47
 draft and, 20–21, 23, 25
 HD in:
  discharge, 44, 45
  Good Conduct Medal, 48
  induction, 25
  See also 1325th Engineer General Service Regiment
 racism in, 25–26, 28–29, 37, 162–163
 HD's strategy toward, 47–49
 reception center at Camp Upton, 25, 27
U.S. Department of Transportation, Consumer Affairs Division, 159–160

U.S. Supreme Court, separate but equal education and, 66–67
United Way of Rockland County, HD as board member, 168
University of Arkansas, 63, 68
University of Brussels, 81
University of Louisville, 56
University of Wisconsin, 56, 98
Urban League Conference, 103

Vietnam war, 98–99, 101
Vincent, Edward, 111
violence by blacks, 100–108
    fostering racism, 100, 102
    futility of, 102
    importance of condemning, 101–102, 107–108
    overshadowing black majority, 105, 107
    promoting white extremist politicians, 102–106
Virginia State College, 111

Walker, Rudolph, 58, 59
Wallace, George, 103, 105–106
Wanamaker, Sam, 26
Ware, Gilbert, 104
Watkins, Thomas, 58, 59
Watson, James "Skiz," 52
Wellesley College, 211
Western Reserve University, 77
White, Vernon, 53
Wilburn, David, 56
Williams School 14, 20
Woodruff, Hale, 51
Woods, Robert, 111
World War II *see* U.S. Army
Wright, Nathan, 132, 140–142
Wright, Richard, 86–87, 133
Wright, Virgil, 76

Yale University, 98, 145
YMCA, Nyack branch, 20
Young, Whitney, 103